THE DEATH OF HUMAN INTERACTION

A Sociologist and Psychologist's Perspective from a Non-Expert in Both Areas

Aaron Panzer

Copyright © 2014 Aaron Panzer

All rights reserved.

ISBN: 0615978703
ISBN 13: 9780615978703
Library of Congress Control Number: 2014904429
Aaron Panzer, San Francisco, CA

Some of the facts might not be true, but the opinions certainly are.

On Oct. 28, 2012, I was confronted with a dilemma that I had so proudly avoided for many years. You see, on that chilly October day, my flip phone screen scrambled into infinite whiteness, compelling me to close it for the last time and forcing me to answer that question that would alter the course of my future: "Do I buy a smart phone?"

Perhaps that sounds a bit dramatic, but consider this: When I was growing up in the late 80s/early 90s, almost no one had a cell phone. There were plenty of other distractions, but none as easily accessible as a smart phone is in today's world. Smart phones, while technological marvels compared with their predecessors from the late 20th century, serve as great interrupters, ones that we seemingly appreciate. According to the Panzer Institute of Market Research, 98 percent of people send at least 700 text messages per day, check Facebook 35 times an hour, and play three hours' worth of Angry Birds (or some other dumb game) a day using their smart phone. However, of the smart phone users that are currently single, 93 percent will get laid only once every two years, primarily due to the fact that since the introduction of the smart phone, interactions amongst strangers has declined 78.39493837 percent. Does my struggle with the dilemma, "Do I buy a smart phone?" seem less dramatic now?

This question, of course, led to my next few questions—all based on the foundation of "Why?" Why do we rely so heavily today on technologies like smart phones that, while impressively transforming the way we communicate, transmute how we relate with one another? Why do we construct virtual barriers and allow them to create real divides? Why does it feel like we *appreciate* these divides? And how (I realize I said this is all about "Why?" but I lied—get used to it; it'll happen more) did we arrive at a point in history where intimacy amongst family, friends, and neighbors is a pastime? To find an answer, I looked to the history and evolution of my own family.

Once upon a time, my father's entire family lived in Philadelphia and my mother's entire family lived in New York City. Both of Jewish descent, their families had similar stories of ancestors (grandparents, great-grandparents, aunts, and uncles) that emigrated from Europe and discovered Jewish communities in their respective cities upon which they could rely as they built their new lives in the United States. For their ancestors, community and, more importantly, family was imperative; they needed one another if they were going to make it in this new land, especially during the Depression and two World Wars.

By the time my parents were born (in the early 1950s), community was still important, but it had become more a cultural imperative than a necessity for survival. Still, seeing their extended family of cousins, aunts, uncles, and grandparents on a regular basis was the norm. They'd do dinners at one another's homes weekly. They'd babysit for each other and help out with their pets. There was never a feeling of loneliness because they were never alone; they always had someone with whom they could talk, which helped create a strong sense of community.

Never being alone, however, was a double-edged sword. Everyone always knew each other's business, whether you wanted it that way or not. Secrets either didn't exist or were hard to keep. Privacy was barely existent as gossip persisted. (It's a cultural imperative for Jews.) While community is a wonderful thing, it's natural for people to stray away from it from time to time.

As my parent's generation grew up and the American middle class really began to prosper, opportunities and needs across the country (and the world) began to explode, from Boston to LA, Miami to Seattle. Colleges also became less exclusive venues and more affordable to the everyman (and woman). All of this led to a great dispersion of people away from their homes and from their communities to chase these new opportunities. As a result, the sense of community that once endured in America has decayed and created a less intimate world.

THE DEATH OF HUMAN INTERACTION

Alright, I'll stop sugarcoating it for you. ... The decline I refer to is worse than I suggest here and will soon lead to a funeral of something very near and dear to us, something that took mankind thousands of years to perfect, something essential to community and based on the foundation of intimacy, something we are close to recklessly throwing away, disregarding it as insignificant, as if it never even mattered in the first place. But, IT DID. It still does. This thing I refer to is *natural human interaction*, the topic of this book (kind of ... the topic of this book is people's addictive and abusive natural instincts as much as anything). The pessimist in me believes that we're on a course we cannot reverse, that we've tasted privacy and appreciate it more than intimacy, that our fate has already been established. The optimist in me ... well, the optimist died while writing this book.

Did I buy a smart phone? Why would I even consider buying a smart phone? What does buying one simple little smart phone have to do with the decline of community and the increased interest in privacy? Where are my pants? Again, for answers to all of your questions (including the one about my pants), please read on!

MY IDEAL WORLD

If I could create my (highly extroverted) ideal world, every person would walk down the street greeting each other with a friendly and sincere "Hello. How are you doing?" No white wires dangle from anyone's ears, hindering the potential for these two people to have a conversation.

In my ideal world, when a family gets home from work and/or school, they are truly home together. The television, video games, and the Internet are powered off and left off. Children play in the backyard then come inside to help their parents prepare food. The parents sass the children and the children provide a fun-loving headache to the parents. After dinner they all play a board or card game together, which the parents win just barely, hoping to not completely crush their children's spirits while maintaining a sense of pride that they can still beat their almost-teenage children in something ... anything. Then, as the children grow, the family often shares in a thought-provoking conversation where the parents are always right (or so they say as they fear they've reached the point in time when their children have gotten smarter and/or less delusional than them).

At work, in meetings, no one from the CEO down is allowed to use a cell phone, Blackberry, iPhone, iPad, Droid, Palm, or any other device that can connect them to a world outside the room. People actually have to pay attention to their colleagues in front of them and the topic of the meeting. I realize it sounds criminal to suggest the creation of a highly efficient environment by way of containing everyone's full attention, but that's just how I roll.

Outside meetings, it's protocol for people to get out of their cubes and offices and physically walk over to have a conversation with the person/people from whom they are seeking information. Not only does this (seemingly creative in this day and age) plan promote one small step in the fight against adult obesity, it also leads to more constructive conversations. People are not allowed to hide behind cube walls and their computers. They have to show their pale, wrinkly, freckly, four-eyed faces to the world.

In school, computers and tablets are set aside or stripped of all applications not useful to the day's lesson plan. There's no *click-clacking* of computers. No web searches. No instant messaging. There's no solitaire, YouTube, Facebook, Twitter, or celebrity gossip.

On the road, people would have to pull over to ask their fellow man (or woman ... I'm no sexist) for directions. If no one's around to guide them, they'd find themselves on an unplanned adventure through the city streets of Boston or the country roads of Wyoming. Yes, it can be stressful to get lost, but sometimes you need to get lost to find what type of person you are. (That ONE philosophy course that I took during college is clearly paying dividends with deep thoughts like this!)

In my ideal world, people are interested in their own lives and not the A-to-D-rate celebrities our society glamorizes. People tell funny or dramatic stories of events they've endured; they share their interests, their feelings, their fears; they get off their butt-indented couches, go out the door, and make a few mistakes. They may cry a few times, but they'll certainly laugh and smile more—exponentially more.

THE DEATH OF HUMAN INTERACTION

In this world, a man has the courage to speak to the woman next to him and maybe ask her out for a cup of coffee, bottle of wine, or a walk in the sun. And the woman has the sensibility to open herself up because—who knows? After all, he's just talking about a simple cup of coffee ... not sex, a relationship, marriage, children, and the whole nine yards. My ideal world encourages a man to meet a woman (or woman to meet a man or a woman to meet a woman or a man to meet a man or whatever other scenario has been legalized recently) in person and have a conversation. If they're both smiling at the end, they'll plan a second conversation a few days later. No one meets over the Internet or hunts the other person down on a social networking site. There is a trust in the air that the person next to you is good and decent, and you would like to see him or her again.

Alas, my ideal world is one of historical fantasy. One day way back before our brains were overloaded with mostly useless information and our bodies overwhelmed with devices, my ideal world existed. There were flaws (e.g., you couldn't watch every single March Madness game live on TV) but people were encouraged to use their minds and to be creative, social, sensual, adventurous. The sad truth is the world I dream of has disappeared forever. Some people call it a technological revolution—a smarter, quicker, more interactive society. I call it the *Death of Human Interaction*. (*Human Interaction is defined by Panzer's Dictionary as real – meaning non-virtual – interpersonal interaction between two human beings – as opposed to orangutans – minus the white noises in life plus ears, minds, hearts, and souls wide open.*)

I once bought entirely into our technologically enhanced society with blind obedience. However, over the years I grew aware of my habits and attempted to claw my way out toward freedom. The journey out of this invisible prison is long and hard, and, while not entirely escapable, I always try. I encourage you to do the same. I would even go so far as to suggest and lead a militant revolution that would destroy all the factories that produce these gadgets and introduce an absolute prohibition on the batteries that power them; but let's be honest,

I'll probably get distracted by SportsCenter tomorrow morning and Facebook in the afternoon. This routine will continue day after day till I'm old, gray, and don't know any better. Instead, just follow these instructions word for word, and you'll be okay:

1. *Buy this book* – Don't just sit and read the book in Barnes & Noble. (I'd also reference Borders, but technology killed them too.) If you can pay five bucks for an over-brewed cup of coffee, you can afford the reasonable $29.95 it will cost you to own this very enlightening book.
2. *Read this book* – Don't read this book with a grain of salt because I'm right. By the end, I'll have you convinced of this. And, if you need more convincing, just look at my picture on the back cover. I look trustworthy, right? (Note to self: Tell publisher to put my picture on the back cover.) If this books ends up as a coaster on your coffee table, you probably didn't follow my instructions.
3. *Don't follow my lead* – At least not regarding the personal stories that I tell throughout the book. These are examples of where I have come from, not where I am going.
4. *Follow my lead* – This may seem contradictory to #3, but it isn't … trust me. (Did you not look at my picture on the back cover yet?) Follow me to the promised land of true human interaction. (For all of you biblical types, my name is that of Moses's brother; hence, I can probably get you there assuming my GPS acquires satellites.) Have conversations and really get to know your fellow people. You'll be surprised what you learn about the people around you and about yourself.
5. *Tell your friends* – Make this the next "must-read" book that you tell all your family and friends about. If you tell five people who tell five people who tell five more people (and on and on), this book will make the best sellers list. (It might make it faster if you tell them through Facebook, but that'd be cheating.) Trust me, this is not a pyramid scheme; it is an investment in your

THE DEATH OF HUMAN INTERACTION

future (spoken like a true pyramid scheme)! You'll want to tell your friends and family so that you have people with whom to go through the lifestyle changes. It is difficult to tackle change alone. Plus, the more people that buy this book, the closer I am to being out of debt (and, if you tell enough friends, perhaps I will make enough money to throw a very large, social, anti-technology party to celebrate … just check your inbox in a few months for the e-vite).

6. *Enjoy*! – This is a very important step that people often forget to do when reading such a (hilarious) book. I promise you will learn to love me by the end.

I hope …

ONE

"The Lost Generation"

Welcome to my book!

For those of you who are new to reading, this is chapter 1. The sequence of this book is numerical, going from low to high and categorized by chapters. If you would like to get a good idea of what this chapter entails, you can either look at the title on the first page of the chapter (as shown above) or view the table of contents. You can find the table of contents a few pages back. (If you reach the front book cover, you've gone too far.)

I've explained the system of this book in such extensive detail for you, the reader, because the primary age demographic of this book I have targeted falls within "The Lost Generation." No, not the generation born during the late 1800s, not those that lived through the Titanic (the real event ... not the movie with Leo and Kate) and fought in World War I (more commonly known today as "There was a world war before the one with the Nazis?").

I think it's funny that authors and historians consider that generation "lost." How can you consider an entire generation "lost" when those who lived during that time did so with a purpose? They saw the turn of the 20th century. They fought for human rights and created labor unions (at a time when unions actually fought to serve the best interests of employees). They fought for women's suffrage. They had a president who created a national park system well before protecting the environment was popular. They were the first ones to drive cars (and didn't have to deal with traffic ... lucky bastards). They were the first to fly airplanes (and their bags were checked for free). They fought and won the "The War to End All Wars" (again, the war before World War II, also previously known as "The Great War," which you sadly may not be aware of as I concluded from my extensive Wikipedia search and discovered there are surprisingly no famous video games based on it).

When I think of the word "lost," I think of those that exist but don't understand—better yet, those that don't even try to understand. Individuals that are lost live by rules they didn't create and decisions they never had the opportunity to influence. Essentially, they act upon what is expected of them because their family or friends or society tells them to, not because it makes sense. This is a direct characterization of my generation, those born between the mid-1970s and early 1990s, not the generation of a hundred years ago ... and it is only getting worse. We are "The Lost Generation," and we are followed by "The Not Found Generation."

Our generation wasn't always this way, and it doesn't have to end as such. There is hope that we can become the "The Not So Lost Generation," but to get there a lot of people will need to make a big effort. The thing is that our generation grew up during one of the greatest technological booms that man has ever experienced. Thirty-five years ago, we had only a few sources of information: network television, radio, and newspapers (and even more at the library if you were willing to get off your ass and get there). Today we have moved far beyond network television (and cable television for that matter) to satellite and digital television—even television provided through the Internet. People have what feels like seven million channels accessible to them via one tiny remote. If they aren't TV watchers, they now have the opportunity to use the Internet for news, information, and entertainment. And the Internet is accessible everywhere, including cellular telephones. On top of that, the old sources of information still exist (at least for now).

With unlimited amounts of information at our fingertips, the questions that we as a whole should ask ourselves (but haven't) are, "What is good information? What sources should we turn to for news? Information? Entertainment? Communication? What is truth vs. fabrication?" People no longer exhibit discretion—they no longer know how to. Because the amount of information out there has become so vast, the line between what is real and what is theater has grown blurry. One top of that, people have begun, more so than ever before, to exhibit serious symptoms of attention deficit disorder (ADD). As such, my generation evolved into "The Lost Generation."

It's ironic that in a world with such incredible technological advances, we as people receded. In our technologically overdeveloped world, things became too easy. In the course of just a few short decades, we no longer feel obligated to be human in the traditional sense of the word. We are excused from face-to-face communication with one another; we don't have to step outside our homes for weeks at a time unless the freezer's empty (and in some cases there are ways to get around that too); and, to go to an extreme example, we don't even have to feel the consequence of killing our fellow man (because that can be done virtually now too).

Today we merely resemble humans of the past; we're desensitized—we're drones. We do have five senses common to the ancestral humans; we can hear, feel, see, taste, and smell (though this is up for debate). However, we have lost certain abilities. We no longer have the ability to reason. Why come to conclusions on your own when someone else can do this for you? Our literacy (and interest in such) is deteriorating. Why exercise your brain when you don't have to? Our sense of exploration and adventure has evaporated. Why travel to Africa when you can watch a documentary about it on Netflix? Worst of all, our ability to interact with those around us has diminished. We have reached the brink of *The Death of Human Interaction*.

For those of you readers born prior to the "The Lost Generation," I have faith that you know how to continue on without following any further directions.

For my fellow "lost" and confused friends, this is the end of chapter 1. As you may infer, this chapter provides an introductory setup for the rest of the book. It is a common trick that authors of these types of books use. Since I am not one to work outside the box, I will play a similar game. I am sorry to be so sneaky so early on, but the good news is there is plenty more to read.

At this point, keep the book open! It is essential that you follow that instruction. If you close it now, you will not know what the subsequent chapters discuss. Now turn to the next page (I'll wait) ...

THE DEATH OF HUMAN INTERACTION

Good! You're learning fast.

That was a test of your listening skills. On one hand, you passed with flying colors; on the other, in following my instructions, you're technically still acting like a drone.

Please continue to the next page for the start of chapter 2, "The Birth of Our Fate ..."

TWO

Birth Of Our Fate

My generation may be lost, but it's not our fault. (On a side note, I commend you for following my instructions from the end of chapter 1. You ARE salvageable!)

The 20th century saw the greatest advancement of communications technology EVER. From the introduction of dialogue in movies to the invention of television, to the first cellular phone, the personal computer and, of course, the Internet, the speed of communication evolved from pony express to high-speed everything in the blink of an eye. Have we peaked? Hell no (but we'll get to that throughout the course of this book)! Before we explore where we are going, it's important to discuss how we got here.

A good author would take the time to do thorough research and craft a very accurate timeline of events that led us to this point. Too bad a good author didn't write this book. (Would you prefer good or honest? Not sure you can have both.) I could rack my brain for months on end; I could endlessly debate my friends over which *ONE* technology sent us down this spiraling path, which *ONE* technology is truly to blame. Where would that leave us? Perhaps in a place where one would argue that the Internet led to information overload and dilution of our brains! But was the Internet the first way to communicate to a mass audience in real time? No, and don't blame television either (although, as you'll read in chapter 3, I personally have plenty for which to blame television)! Does anyone remember radio? Granted, it was a form of communication that relied more heavily on the use of your ears than more prevalent technologies of today (communications judged by today's standards *absolutely suck* unless there is some form of visual imagery), but it could send information far and wide instantaneously. Or one could go back even farther in time and blame our fate on the printing press. How else were we first able to find a way to deliver information in general to a mass audience?

In the end, the channels/vehicles of communication that led us to this point don't matter quite as much as the will of the people using them. For example, the inherent fact is, for a person born in 1982 (conveniently me), televisions, radio, newspapers, computers, mobile phones, etc. already existed and were on their way to driving *The Death of Human Interaction*. As our will was tested, did we deny these technologies? Quite the contrary—we embraced them. And, for a person born in 2012, so many forms of distraction already exist that, in my opinion, their will doesn't stand a chance. They will be pushed farther over the edge into the great abyss of communication degradation.

The most important part of this discussion to understand is perspective. I, a person born in 1982, believe the world that is *supposedly* heading toward "improved communication" by way of the Internet, mobile phones, and social networking is actually moving toward shallower, more voluminous relationships (it is about quantity over quality), but I may be an outlier. A person born in 1952 may view the world as a place that used to value in-person community and doesn't understand the notion of virtual community. And a person born in 2012 may know a completely different world. ... They may see the world that came before them, especially the past 30 years, as a place that evolved into simpler, more technologically enhanced and efficient methods of communication; they may fear what's next or they may embrace it. Or the world may already be so long gone at the time of their birth that they don't/won't have a clue!

THE DEATH OF HUMAN INTERACTION

When considering *The Death of Human Interaction*, our fate can be compared to an Olympic relay race. Imagine you are the second or third runner out of four. You didn't start the race and you won't finish the race. You are the one taking the baton and moving forward in time. Every step you take has implications as to where you will go and how it will shape the race. Each of us was born into a world presently defined in a way that was dictated long before we took our first breath. We cannot control what came before us or how the world embraced or dismissed it. We can, however, control how we each individually respond to it.

Communications technology, at one point in time, provided value to our lives. As these technologies evolved over time or new ones replaced old ones, more value was provided. However, at some juncture, we reached the tipping point; our world moved from creating technologies that provide value to developing technologies that are simply "cool." I challenge you to remove the blinders and ask yourself what communications technologies truly provide value to your life (day-to-day, month-to-month, or year-to-year) and which ones are simply "cool."

While you ask yourself that question, go on to chapter 3 and read about my greatest childhood addiction, the technology that was simply "cool" throughout my formative years ... TELEVISION!

THREE

Confessions Of A Recovering Television Addict

Before we go too far on this journey together, I think it is important that you understand that I am not some self-righteous asshole. I am not perfect, and, without a doubt, I will prove myself to be a hypocrite several times throughout this book. (I will elaborate on this in chapter 40.) For example, I probably spent 90-95 percent of my childhood watching television (give or take 60 percent).

When I was seven years old, my parents gave my brother, Jeff, the best gift of all ... his own bedroom. You see, my older brother, whom I looked up to oh so dearly, asked them to kick me out onto the streets and leave me to fend for myself. Then he would be the youngest member of the family once again and get the attention he used to get before I was born. My parents thought a fair compromise would be just to move me into the guest bedroom. Looking back on this, I think they acted fairly. I would, however, miss the late night conversations after we were put to bed—conversations that involved me babbling and Jeff telling me to shut up 'cause he was trying to sleep. Jeff always valued a good night's sleep. I always valued a late night. He especially hated that I would put the television on to fall to sleep. He preferred ABSOLUTE silence.

For the first few months of living on my own, I felt highly offended (as much as a seven-year-old could feel highly offended). We would still pass in the hall, see each other at the dinner table, play sports in the backyard and video games in the basement, but those were months with space between us and an abstract level of emptiness within me. I couldn't tell what I missed most—me babbling on for hours at night, the satisfaction I got from driving my big brother to the edge, or the television. I think I probably missed the television the most. Oh, the television …

Then, for my eighth birthday, my parents came up with a solution that would remedy all the disdain I felt toward him … they bought me my own personal television. Wow! was I excited for this gift. (For my sake, please reread this sentence in Christopher Walken's voice.)

"You mean, I can lock myself in my bedroom and watch whatever shows I want to all day long?"

My parents' response was always, "Yep."

(This was way cooler than using one of the other six televisions around the house—where only five people lived. With any one of those, someone could enter the room and ask to change the channel on me. Then what would I have done?)

"But you have to be responsible," they would add. "If you act naughty, we'll take away your television privileges for a couple days." (I should note that taking away my privileges meant hiding my remote control in my father's night table drawer and unplugging the television, both impossible obstacles to overcome when I decided to disobey my punishment.)

I would promise them I would be good … and I was (almost) always good. If there was one thing I didn't want to lose, it was my television privileges. In hindsight, buying a television and putting it my room was probably one of the worst things my parents ever did for me.

THE DEATH OF HUMAN INTERACTION

After I hooked up that beautiful 13-inch color box of television, I developed a new routine. Every single day I rushed home from school, ran right up to my room, locked the door, opened up my backpack, and supposedly got cracking on my homework for the night. It typically took me anywhere from six to eight hours a night to fill out one simple multiplication table and write five lines of cursive. You must understand; it's not that I was a slow child. I simply did other things in between: I took bathroom and food breaks. My afternoon snack of Doritos, Ruffles, and Swedish Fish always came at 4:30 p.m., dinner was at 6 p.m., and dessert was around 7:30 p.m. Sometimes I showered at night. Oh yeah, and the television was obviously always on.

That year also marked another major milestone in my young life: A wonderful entertainment company that you may have heard of called the Disney Corporation revolutionized the American afternoon television schedule when it created The Disney Afternoon, a two-hour television block consisting of some of the best of Disney's cartoon series.

I had the schedule down pat. During that first year, *The Adventures of the Gummi Bears* started at 3 p.m. and was followed by *Duck Tales*, *Chip 'n Dale Rescue Rangers*, and *Tale Spin*. I always missed the first 15 minutes of *Gummi Bears* because I was a slow walker, and I was busy talking to my friends about the upcoming excitement on the television that awaited me back home. It was a sacrifice I was willing to make—I felt some contempt toward *Gummi Bears* because my oldest brother, Marc (my greatest childhood torturer … our relationship will further be explored in a book of its own), loved it. *Chip 'n Dale Rescue Rangers* was my favorite show. When I grew up, I wanted to be a fun-loving chipmunk with a red nose solving crimes and wearing Hawaiian shirts, much like Dale. (I still yearn for that life.)

Then came year two. Disney used a group of high-level intelligence experts to concoct a plan to further commit a generation of unsuspecting children to watching television. They bumped each show up a half hour and created a new show, *Darkwing Duck*, for the 4:30 p.m. timeslot. (*Darkwing Duck* may have been even better than *Rescue Rangers*!) This would be a recurring theme from season to season of the Disney Afternoon, and my biggest concern that year was that I might miss the first 15 minutes of *Duck Tales* each day. I would know how each caper ended, but clueless how it began. How did they find themselves in that debacle? Did Uncle Scrooge provoke the situation? Was it Huey, Dewey, and Louie's fault? Launchpad's? Who wants to live in a world of unknowns like that? Certainly not me. I think I got fairly skinny that year as I would sprint home from school each day to make sure I didn't miss a moment. This was one of the truly great challenges of my childhood.

A reader of this might suggest that The Disney Corporation stole my childhood afternoons away from me, that Michael Eisner and his bastard minions are all to blame! That's actually true. The Disney Corporation did steal my childhood afternoons away from me. Then sitcoms stole my evenings and nights, whether it was re-runs from 5 to 8 p.m. or primetime television from 8 to 11 p.m. At one point in my life, I could probably recite the scripts for certain episodes for such shows as *Full House, Family Matters, Saved by the Bell, The Fresh Prince of Bel-Air, The Cosby Show, The Brady Bunch,* and *Gilligan's Island*. One might consider this to be a sad fact, but I ... well, yes, it is sad.

While I did get my homework done each night and get good grades, sometimes I stop to wonder about the memories I may have missed out on and the friendships I could have had. As a child, I had an addiction in the strictest sense of the word, and there are still days when I relapse (which has happened quite often through the course of writing this book, but let's justify it by calling it research). On those days, the addiction prevails. But I am stronger and more aware today than I was as a child. I don't have to live my life vicariously through stories drafted by screenwriters and told by actors. I have a fully functioning body, a desire to experience, and a strong will.

THE DEATH OF HUMAN INTERACTION

The mixed emotions I felt from watching fictional characters stumble through life could never match those I have felt as I have made my own stories and had my own personal adventures and mishaps that can serve a lifetime of smiles and tears.

In retrospect, one of the worst requests I may have ever made was to get a television for my eighth birthday. One of the worst actions I may have ever made was plugging it in and turning it on. Conversely, some of the best actions of my life were those that caused me to get grounded (e.g., the hit and run when I was 16, the times I got caught drinking, etc.) because not only were they real experiences of mine that taught me life lessons (and serve as good stories today), they also forced my parents to fulfill their promise to unplug my television from the wall and stash my remote in my father's nightstand drawer. One of the greatest regrets I have is allowing television to steal some of the best moments of my childhood.

Don't feel sorry for me. I am more to blame than anyone. In my defense, those shows were pretty badass for a pre-teen.

FOUR

Galvin-izing Your Ride

Watching television serves as a great mechanism for planning to be antisocial. If you want to be antisocial on the fly, there is nothing better than the original "shut-up" device ... the car radio!!

In the early 1930s, the Galvin Corporation, which was owned by the infamous Galvin brothers, Paul V. and Joseph E., did for the car radio what Thomas Edison did for the light bulb—they invented it. Well, honestly, there is no factual evidence that declares the Galvin brothers the inventors of the car radio (at least according to Wikipedia); however, they were the first to commercially manufacture and sell the fitted car radio. With the success garnered from the introduction of the fitted car radio, the Galvin Corporation grew to proportions similar to that of an organization like Motorola. Actually, the Galvin Corporation (as I'm certain you don't recognize their name) changed its name to Motorola when it started manufacturing car radios.

Between the two brothers, Paul was the real visionary although he credits Joseph as being an equal part of that vision. He was once quoted as saying, "It just came to me one day. Joey was blabbering on about Hoover. He was blaming Hoover for the Depression or something like that. That was when the song 'Dream a Little Dream of Me' came into my head. I started tuning him out and thought, man, there has got be a more effective way to tune this damn liberal out more often. And the rest is history!"

In the U.S. today, almost every car that exists has some form of a car radio as part of a greater stereo system. It all started with the radio, then it moved to the 8-track, cassette player, CD player, satellite radio, and MP3 player. Today, cars have more technology in them than my grandparents' house ever did. Oh yes, there are so many ways to distract yourself, to steal your attention from the traffic all around, the raccoon darting into the street (soon-to-be roadkill), or the pedestrian crossing the street directly in front of you (also soon-to-be roadkill). It makes driving that much more exciting.

Some cars these days even have televisions and DVD players in them (hopefully showing *Disney Afternoon* videos), which are great for shutting your children up. We have all known or been that noisy obnoxious kid that drives their parent to the brink of insanity while driving from home to school or vice versa. For decades parents struggled to find a way to quiet their children or shut them up entirely without doing something that would have Child Protective Services knocking on their door. Sometime within the past decade, parents determined that the in-car television and DVD player was that silver bullet. The problem? I don't think most parents realize the silver bullet could actually end up shutting their children up for good. Did you know that in-car DVD players can kill a child in a crash at only 18 mph? Apparently the DEKRA Technology Centre in Germany simulated a collision at 18 mph and found that a DVD monitor strapped to the seat's headrest by a belt came loose and went flying into the head of the crash-test dummy sitting in the child-safety seat. But, hey ... isn't that a risk that most parents are willing to take in order to get a little piece of mind in the car? In this case the "death of human interaction" might simply end up being "death"!

But it doesn't have to stop there! Not only are you willing to put your children's lives at risk, you are also such a selfless individual that you welcome the idea putting other drivers' lives at risk by allowing them to get equally distracted by your televisions set. I know I personally would rather get distracted by the visual image of Teletubbies being broadcast from your minivan driving in front of me than pay attention to the hazards on the road. (I should note that I am a risk seeker!) Thank you for sharing the deathly adventure just because you are too weak to deal with your screaming children. One question: Did you ever stop to think that your kids are screaming (a) because you never give them enough attention, or (b) because you spoil them so rotten with things like electronics in the car that they feel like they always deserve more? My advice? Grow a pair, get rid of the in-car television and DVD player, and give your kids real attention that could lead to a REAL bond between child and parent.

In my opinion, despite the risk of death, the car radio and everything subsequently associated with it is a great thing, and its greatness is not weighed solely on the guilty pleasures, like Celine Dion or Miley Cyrus, which you get to indulge in every time you take a ride. Instead, its great-i-tude is based on its being a medium of indirect communication. For example, I could be driving along with 2008 Noble Prize-winning physicist Makoto Kobayashi with the music blaring. Suddenly Noble Prize-winning physicist Makoto Kobayashi starts to explain his work on CP-violation and his "discovery of the origin of the broken symmetry which predicts the existence of at least three families of quarks in nature" (much like you, I have no idea what CP-violation is) but, because of the volume of the music, it is nearly impossible to hear his explanation.

At this point, I have a choice: (a) continue to listen to the music, drowning out Nobel Prize-winning physicist Makoto Kobayashi, or (b) turn the volume down in order to hear his super-duper intriguing theorem. Well, of course I reach toward the volume dial and turn it WAY down because I want to learn everything there is to learn about CP-violation (whatever the hell that is). Using the car radio as a medium, I have indirectly signified two things to Nobel Prize-winning physicist Makoto Kobayashi: (1) I respect Noble Prize-winning physicist Makoto Kobayashi, and (2) I truly care about what Nobel Prize-winning physicist Makoto Kobayashi has to say.

On the other hand, the car radio can be used to send negative messages. In a similar scenario, let's replace Nobel Prize-winning physicist Makoto Kobayashi with my student teacher from second grade, Miss Wallace. Oh man, Miss Wallace USED TO BE so hot, but the years have not been good to her, and her voice hardly sounds as sexy as I remember. She used to have a Demi Moore-like voice; now she sounds more like Harvey Fierstein. She is carrying on about the new wallpaper she just put up in her den when the radio catches my ear; the song "Moving in Stereo" (by The Cars) from *Fast Times at Ridgemont High* comes on, and I start thinking about Phoebe Cates in her red bikini. Then I start fantasizing about the Miss Wallace of twenty years ago, but the fantasy isn't strong yet. The wallpaper obsessed, modern-day Miss Wallace keeps yammering. I have to find a way to drown her out. So, almost in slow motion, I extend my right hand out toward the volume knob on the radio and turn the volume WAY up. She ignores it and keeps yapping. So, I turn it up again to the point where our ears almost bleed. She finally gets the message that I don't care about wallpaper; in fact, I've never cared about wallpaper. I just wish she would shut up, and she does. FINALLY, I am left in peace with my fantasy of the Miss Wallace of old. The Galvin brothers saved my day.

In this scenario, by turning up the volume of the car radio, I indirectly expressed that: (1) I don't care about wallpaper, (2) I don't care what Miss Wallace has to say, (3) I hardly respect the person sitting directly next to me, and (4) I'm a coldhearted bastard. The Miss Wallace scene was an extreme scenario that may have included a few "slight" fabrications. Regardless, it demonstrates how technology gets in the way of natural human interaction. I chose radio, a piece of technology (and all its wonders), over a living, breathing human being sitting directly next to me. What does that say about me? Oh yeah … "I'm a coldhearted bastard." No! That is not what it means. It indicates that I am an active participant in our modern society where electronic technologies have a strong presence; most of the time, much like all of you, I hardly even realize it.

Think about it. How many times have you turned the volume up on the car radio while someone else was talking? We've all done it at some point; we simply either don't recognize or choose to ignore the message(s) we send to our fellow man when we do. And, if we wish to pass blame (also a favorite American pastime), we can always blame the Galvins! (Is anyone up for a class action law suit against Motorola or, better yet, Google as they now own Motorola?)

I have mixed feelings about the Galvins. On one hand, they commercialized a technology that thrives by interrupting conversation and thought. On the other, there is nothing more fun than rocking out to Whitney Houston—excuse me, Guns & Roses—while driving! Without the Galvins, the second would not be possible.

FIVE

Thank You, Martin Cooper!

The car radio might have been the original "shut up" device, but it is certainly not the most prevalent, at least not anymore.

If there is one day that should forever be remembered (though it is often forgotten) as a day that changed the course of human history, it should be April 3, 1973. On that day, Martin Cooper, an inventor, researcher, and executive with Motorola, made the first phone call from a handheld mobile telephone. That historic phone call was placed to his rival, Dr. Joel S. Engel of Bell Labs, with no intention whatsoever of bragging. ... Okay, yes, the phone call was made with the malicious intent to brag. Fortunately for Mr. Cooper, frustrating mobile carriers that often drop calls (like Verizon does to me) did not yet exist. Unfortunately, however, call waiting had not yet been invented, so Cooper eagerly called back 35 times over the course of two hours, each time receiving a busy signal while Dr. Engel spoke with customer service from his long-distance provider regarding the issues he was having with his service. Cooper finally got through on lucky try number 36, and the boasting began. (For Dr. Engel, he was confused as he thought it was an April Fools' Day joke two days late.)

April 3, 1973, was a turning point in the history of natural human interaction, for that day led to the car phone, then the cell phone, then the smart phone. The birth of the mobile phone gave people many new methods they could use to put themselves in danger while driving and to ignore others sitting directly in front of them in any and every setting; people no longer had to limit themselves to acting oblivious only in their living rooms while using their landlines.

I'd like to think that when Martin Cooper invented the mobile phone, he gave the human race the benefit of the doubt, that he believed we have manners and lack ADHD. I imagine he thought the mobile phone had a terrific functional purpose, which it has. The mobile phone made it much easier to connect with others. I highly doubt, however, that he ever envisioned the mobile phone becoming the center of people's livelihoods, that people would feel incomplete without it, or that it would become the great distracter in our lives that it has become.

Yes, as I mentioned, the cell phone can serve a great purpose. For example, when I first got my driver's license, my parents got me a cell phone for emergency purposes. They told me that a sixteen-year-old boy can be irresponsible from time to time, especially behind the wheel (a theory I proved true a number of times), and that having a cell phone handy would be invaluable. What they didn't tell me was that two years later, when I started college in Syracuse two hours away from home, my cell phone would be the perfect way for my mother to check in with me regarding everything.

I got telephone calls in the morning to tell me what the weather in Syracuse was going to be like that day and that I should dress warm (as if the snow outside wasn't a good enough indicator). Then, my mother would call me during the day to make sure I wasn't getting into trouble or to tell me what one of my brothers did or what my father hit with his car. (I should note that my father is a terrible driver—watch out if you ever see a bald-headed man with glasses driving an Acura on the roads of San Diego where my parents currently live.) In the evening, she would call me to see how my day went and complain about the way my father chewed his food during dinner. Since I was her youngest child, I got to hear it all (and still do)! Thank you, Martin Cooper!

I don't want to peg my mother as the only abusive cell phone user in my family. My father often calls to tell me that the dog told him, "I miss Aaron" (which I can totally understand), that he ate strawberries that afternoon, or even just to chew his food while on the phone and prove my mom right on that point.

Also, I used to be a pretty bad cell phone user. When I lived in Los Angeles, I called my friends back on the East Coast all the time and either pulled them into long, torturous conversations while they were in the middle of something important or I would leave long, obnoxious voicemails. In my defense, because LA traffic sucks, I spent a lot of time by myself driving to and from work on a daily basis.

The type of power that the mobile phone has is truly amazing. When I was growing up, hardly anyone had one. People had to make plans with each other before leaving the house. If you weren't the type of person to plan out your day, you were screwed! But that's the way it was, and we all managed okay. In algebra class, if you wanted to pass love letters to your girlfriend, you actually had to hand write them, pass the notes along, and risk the wrong person reading your message. It could always lead to a miscommunication, an embarrassing moment, or a kick to the groin (which happened to me only once), but the adventure was always worth the risk.

Today people can plan on the go. For example, if I am driving home from work and my friend Anthony calls to tell me that he is heading to happy hour where that hot bartender works, I will veer my car in that direction so quickly it will leave skid marks on the road, making plans on the go. If someone needs to get a hold of me in case of an emergency, like their car stalled or they broke their arm, they can reach me. If my family or friends whom I haven't spoken with in a while because I live at least 1,000 miles away want to say "hello," they can more easily access me. And, that accessibility is only increasing. (*I'll discuss this further in Chapter 9.*)

The power of the mobile phone, despite all its beneficial purposes, also acts a divide. It starts with the fact that people have the ability to either answer or ignore other people's phone calls; answering or ignoring people's calls indicates a strong hidden innuendo. To the ones placing the call, if they are ignored and they know your habits, it can create a great deal of anxiety. For example, I know that my wife always has her phone on her with the ringer at full blast. When she doesn't answer my call the first time and it doesn't go straight to voicemail (indicating a dead battery), I assume she is busy with something. When I try again 15 minutes later with still no answer, I start freaking out and thinking the worst. "Where's Katie? She's the one person that's never supposed to screen my calls. She left work two hours ago and should be home by now! Should I start calling the hospitals? Oh, God! Did something happen to her? If something happened to her, how am I ever going to explain it to her parents? Katie, please, please, please answer the phone!" After six more attempts to reach her in a matter of three minutes, I am scared out of my mind but trying to act tough. Then, five minutes later she finally calls me to let me know she was busy getting a manicure and couldn't get to her phone. At this point, I am: (1) thrilled she is alive and well, and (2) upset she disregarded our agreement that she wouldn't spend money on manicures for a while. But I am willing to forgive number 2 considering number 1.

For the people standing by or hanging out with the person receiving the call, if the phone is answered, it's an immediate signal that the people with you are not as important as the person on the phone—not that I'm bitter about it, but come on. Is that person really more entertaining to talk with than me? We've all been guilty party of disrespecting friends at one time or another. Answering your phone in front of others is a commonly accepted—but rude—gesture that demonstrates a lack of manners.

THE DEATH OF HUMAN INTERACTION

My mother (I will make it up to her for using her as an example after she reads this book) is a prime example of the latter. She often begs and pleads with me, "her little baby," to come home for a visit. She misses me so much and CANNOT wait to see me. It is always a great feeling to know that your mother loves you very much, and I love her. But, when I get home, her addiction to her cell phone takes over. My father, whom I also love very much, is not the easier parent to have a cohesive conversation with. A conversation with him can be compared to a conversation with a toddler blurting out any random word or thought that pops into his head. Hence, I have to rely on my mother to entertain me.

My mother, Lori Panzer, is a champion talker. So you'd imagine we would have wonderful conversations during each visit. Not the case. My mother often chooses to talk on the phone with my brother Marc, who is in San Francisco, instead of with the in-person, in-the-flesh me, Aaron, her son sitting directly in front of her. In her defense, I will say that this habit did not begin with the invention of the mobile phone. She used to use the phone to ignore my brothers and me all the same when we were growing up; the difference then was that she had only a landline, meaning there were limits to when and where she could ignore us. Today, because she can take her cell phone EVERYWHERE, she can ignore us in the car, at a restaurant, on a walk, while grocery shopping, etc.

I view my mom's addiction to her cell phone from two different angles. On one hand, it is frustrating as hell. Since I get to see her rarely, it'd be great to be able to have an in-depth conversation with her and not have to learn how to work the XM radio in her car or memorize the menu at P.F. Chang's while she talks on her phone. On the other hand, it serves to remind me that I want to make my cell phone a minimal part of my life. I want to call people when I need to, but I want to be with the people, both physically AND mentally, that are standing right in front of me.

One of the things that I love about traveling abroad is not having a cell phone in my pocket or in my hand. I love that feeling of being disconnected from the world. Cell phones make me feel like I MUST call or text people if I have nothing else to do in order to avert boredom. When I don't have my cell phone, I feel like I embrace the people and the world around me to a greater extent and, ironically, never get bored; I live much more in the moment.

Most people believe that a cell phone is a necessity in our lives the way that food is. Is it really though? I am asking you, Martin Cooper.

SIX

No Seriously ... Thank You, Martin Cooper!

Welcome to the cell phone addendum. It relays the experience and thoughts that I had as I faced THE DEATH OF HUMAN INTERACTION via the cell phone medium.

In my opinion, cell phones create more opportunity for a divide in natural human interactions than anything else. A prime example occurred last night when one of my coworkers displayed some unfortunate habits. While driving back from a work trip, three people were in the car, two of my female coworkers and me. As we got to a point about an hour away from home, one of my coworkers got a phone call from her husband. Without even asking either of us if we minded if she answered the phone while we sat in a small enclosed space, she did. Because we had been away for a few days, if she had been considerate and asked, we gladly would have obliged. But she didn't. And, as kind, respectful people, my other coworker and I turned the radio completely off and sat quietly so that she could hear her husband through the phone.

In general, I'm a very easygoing person with very few pet peeves, and even when someone hammers at one of those pet peeves, I generally stay quiet and just let the situation work itself out. In this situation, I did just that. However, as I sat there quietly, I thought about the situation in which I found myself. My coworker spoke to her husband, whom she would see in about an hour, for 10-15 minutes about the nothings of what went on throughout the day. Of those 10-15 minutes, she even spent one minute talking to her dog through the phone. (I am the self-proclaimed, biggest dog lover in the world, but I think it's ridiculous when people try to talk to their dog through the phone.)

During this time, two other people (if you do the math, you'll realize that is one more person than the number of people talking on the phone in this car) are expected to sit there quietly. Two other people are meant to put their conversation, their thoughts, their ideas, their jokes, their laughs, their everything on hold so that one person can have a completely irrelevant conversation with another person not currently in their presence that they will see in about an hour. Does this situation seem backwards to anyone else? Twenty years ago, this situation never would have occurred! The three people driving in the car would have no one else to talk with while sitting in the car except one another. But, because everyone today has a cell phone (in some cases two or three), the opportunity exists to make conversation with people not currently present instead of those that are.

My recommendation to anyone that reads this book is to think about your setting, the situation you are in, before you pick up the phone and call someone. Realize that you are not the only person in the world and not everyone wants to listen to one side of your conversation (as they can't hear what the person on the other end of the phone is saying … most of the time). Understand that when you pick up the phone in a friend or coworker's presence, you are often signaling to that person to shut up (whether you're doing it intentionally or unintentionally). That is just plain rude and unfair. But I guess life can be unfair sometimes.

Yet again, thank you, Martin Cooper!

THE DEATH OF HUMAN INTERACTION

Trust me—I'm really not an angry person, but I do believe in manners. I use Martin Cooper as a bit of a scapegoat for my anger; however, Martin Cooper IS the inventor of the first successfully operational cellular phone, a device that has grown into the most widely accepted technological excuse for being rude to your fellow man ever invented.

SEVEN

The Zack Morris Impact

Addendum to Cell Phone Chapters

Martin Cooper isn't the only reason that cell phones have become what they are today. Pop culture must share some blame ...

When I was growing up, there were a few celebrities that my friends and I idolized and wished to emulate. I am proud to say that none of my childhood heroes came from a place called *90210*. No ... my heroes lived closer to the *Bayside*. And, of those heroes, there was no one cooler than Zack Morris.

Zack had it all (minus A.C. Slater's Jerry curls). His girlfriend was the head cheerleader, Kelly Kapowski; his best friend, a brainiac named Screech. He practically ran Bayside High, and he did it looking cooler than anyone else, wearing bright (often neon), multicolored outfits. He even had Principal Richard Belding wrapped around his finger. However, nothing was more "rad" about Zack than his cell phone; it was the pinnacle of his popularity. Every kid in America that grew up watching *Saved by the Bell* dreamt of one day owning the sleek, brick-sized *Zack Morris* cell phone. I mean, if you were able to convince your parents to get you one of those, you would surely be the Zack Morris of your school.

Having a *Zack Morris* cell phone meant that you could skip class or, if you decided to attend, be the class clown. It was guaranteed to get you women that would make even Rob Lowe, Kirk Cameron, or Joey Lawrence jealous. And you could do all sorts of other fun stuff, such as call the school principal from the bathroom disguising your voice as a sick teacher cancelling the test that day. (Yes, I have seen every episode of *Saved by the Bell* way too many times. But in my defense, please refer back to chapter 3, "Confessions of a Recovering Television Addict.")

To be honest, Zack Morris was a little ahead of his time. Most people, let alone teenagers, did not have a cell phone until the late 1990s or early 2000s. To see someone walking around with a cell phone similar to the way Zack did during the early '90s (when the show aired) would have been highly unusual. However, it is relevant to credit the impact Zack Morris had on my generation. Visually witnessing someone your age, especially someone "cool," have and use a cell phone made a generation of children and teenagers both consciously and unconsciously want to have one. Some may have viewed it as a practical device; for others it was likely just fun technology. Regardless, Zack Morris helped adapt a generation of youths, and Mark-Paul Gosselaar (the actor who played Zack), should receive royalties from Verizon, AT&T, Sprint, and T-Mobile for the rest of his life for the service he provided their industry.

Or, at very least, the creators of Saved by the Bell *should receive royalties and angry letters from parents all over the world for being part of the cause and not part of the solution!*

EIGHT

Text Messaging: The Good, The Bad, And The ... That's All

If you think that sending and receiving calls are the only disruptions that cell phones cause, you may have just woken up from a coma that you fell into during the mid-1990s; if that's the case, please read on. This will be very useful information for you ...

As I sit at a table in a coffee shop struggling to write this chapter, trying to figure out the right words to use to discuss "text messaging" without being overly redundant of the facts (opinions) I will point out, I decide to solicit some help. At the table next to me are two girls discussing the sorely addictive power of Twitter. Being the shameless person that I am, I interrupt to inform them that I am busy writing a book that relates to their feelings (plus some). I tell them they are not alone, not at all, and I will bring them salvation. (Not really, but it sounds cool, right?)

As our brief interaction winds down, I inform them of my writer's block. I could tell by the looks on their faces that they didn't care yet they were willing to help. So, I asked them, "How do you feel about text messaging?" They blurted out two very different opinions ...

Girl #1 told me, "I hate to talk on the phone. I have to talk on the phone for conference calls on a daily basis and it's exhausting. Then, I have to schedule time to talk to my family every week. Text messaging makes communication quick, easy, and painless. When I already log so many hours on the phone during the day, it's refreshing not to have to do much to communicate." Despite the fact that it felt weird to me (and I pointed this out to her) that she had "to schedule time to talk to [her] family every week," I can relate in some regard. My job demands that I speak to many different people. Then, of course, my Jewish mother loves to talk to her baby boy over the phone. Combined, those two obligations alone can wear the strongest person down.

Girl #2 told me that it kills dating. I thought this was an interesting initial reaction and one I think I understand, but because I've been in a serious relationship for a few years, I asked her to elaborate. She happily explained that text messaging is an easy way out of actually getting to know someone. (Of course, I could argue that using a cell phone in general creates that barrier.) She went on to say that people get so busy that they use it as an excuse to have a conversation without having a conversation, to continue to get to know someone without putting the work into it. Then she voiced her frustration with trying to interpret the tone of someone's text message and leaving the communication between two people to a best guess or an interpretation. "Is the person sending the text message being sarcastic or sincere, coy or bold, playful or mean?" I agreed with her; all of these are up for interpretation, especially when you are just in the process of getting to know someone.

The thing is, they're both right. In a world filled with overabundance IN EVERY REGARD, text messaging gives us the option to communicate painlessly, to operate a bit more efficiently. For example, when I want to get five to ten friends together at the last minute for happy hour, it certainly is easier for me to send out a text message blast to a bunch of people and deal with the follow-up text message conversations in order to coordinate the outing. The same thing goes when I am trying to organize sports. In general, by using text messaging, this type of work can take up 15 minutes of my time. Without text messaging, I would probably have to spend somewhere between an hour and hour and a half of my time calling people and speaking with them, time that I just don't have.

On the other hand, text messaging can be a weak form of communication. With text messaging, it's not always clear what the real message is that someone is trying to send. Text messaging can communicate words (kind of), but it cannot represent tone or demonstrate body language. It is communication with holes. Hence, I have a proposal for all of you ...

My proposal is that you take the time to understand the benefits of text messaging vs. phone vs. in-person conversation. Understand that if you are trying to coordinate schedules, arrange a meeting place, or tell someone that you're on your way, it is okay to use text messaging; in fact, it makes sense! But please don't abuse it. Text messaging is not a good way to get to know someone, have a deep conversation, or negotiate a peace treaty.

On top of all of this, I want you to take a course in text messaging etiquette. (I don't think this course actually exists, but for the right price I will create and teach it.) Is it polite to send or read text messages while having an in-person conversation with another human being? It is sad if you don't know the answer to that—of course it is not polite, dummy! Is it alright to curse or use derogatory language in a text message? Only if you want written proof of a communication that can come back to bite you in the ass. Is it acceptable to hijack a friend or family member's cell phone and send ridiculous messages to many of the contacts in their contact list? This one I am actually okay with as long as you understand the possibility of retaliation. (Someone needs to explain this to my brother, Jeff. Jeff, you must learn that if you are going to give it, you must also be willing to take it!)

Long story short? Don't be a schmuck! Text messaging is now engrained in our society, so learn some damn etiquette! But text messaging isn't the end of it. Thanks to smart phones, now you can also e-mail, Facebook, Tweet, surf the Internet, Skype, and everything else you can imagine from your smart phone, and 99.99999999 percent of people now have them. (My 86-year-old grandmother is part of the 0.00000001 percent that doesn't.)

NINE

Smart Phones: Bringing The World To Utter Demise

I have nothing bad to say about smart phones. No, no ... that's a lie. I have SO MANY bad things to say about smart phones! (You probably could have guessed that based on the title of this chapter if you are at least as perceptive as a goldfish!) If you are reading this book on one of those types of devices, it is possible that you might get a little offended by this chapter (unless you actually have at least a minor sense of humor). If you are reading this as an actual, real, physical book like those found during your great-great-grandparents' day, you might agree with much of the chapter. To find out, read on ...

Over the past several years (until recently), I have been most criticized for not having a smart phone. Coincidentally, over the past several years (until recently), I took the most pride in the fact that I still used a flip phone. (I should clarify for anyone that knows me personally who may be reading this book, even though we all know it is highly unlikely anyone other than my future kids [whom I will force] will read this book ... I did have a Blackberry for work for several years through the final years of my flip-phone days, but it was handed to me at someone else's request Day One at my current company. I never carried it with me outside work and never used it for personal reasons other than to check the scores of Mets and Syracuse basketball games like any good sports fan would. Besides, many people don't even consider a Blackberry to be a real smart phone.)

The smart phone has been integrated into most of our lives the way peanut butter was once upon a time integrated into mine: I could probably live without it, but I sure as hell don't want to. Every which way you turn you see dozens of people (at least) playing with their iPhone, Android, Blackberry, etc. In some cases, they are using it for something relevant (e.g., looking up the score of the Mets or Syracuse basketball game), but in most cases they are not. More often than not, they are Facebooking or YouTubing or Pinteresting or Instagraming or Yelping or (insert any other website that has branded itself into a verb in recent years). Within 20 years, we went from a time when most people didn't even have Internet in their households to dial-up connections to broadband connections to wireless connections to mobile connections. And where has it left us? DISTRACTED!

How many times in the past few years have you been in a conversation with someone that lasted longer than a minute before that person stopped to check their phone for something not very urgent? (I am watching someone across the street from the café where I am presently writing do this as I type.) How many times in the past few years have you been in a conversation that lasted longer than a minute with someone who did not stop to check their phone for something not very urgent? I guarantee that the volume of occurrences for the former are so vast that they all blend into one another, and I guarantee that the few occurrences of the latter stand out in your mind as times where you felt like the other person was fully engaged. The funny (yet sad) thing is that the former has become so normal that checking or playing with your phone in front of another person isn't even considered rude anymore. It has become widely accepted that a person or event happening outside your proximity can be more relevant than the people or things within your proximity and it is okay to divert your attention away. For once, I am stymied as to why this is so. If anyone else can enlighten me, please shoot me a text message and I will pause the conversation I am in at that moment to read your thoughts.

When I think of smart phones, a few questions come to mind:

- *Why is it that we even want a magical little machine in our hand or in our pocket all the time?* Because "it makes life easier"? What is the definition of "easier" anyway? If "easier" means providing people the opportunity to communicate at a high level with every single person around the world at the speed of light (assuming you can get a signal), then yes, it does make life easier. (Who really wants to be connected at the speed of light all the time? Apparently everyone but my grandmother, but she also doesn't really know what a smart phone is.) If "easier" means bringing people together to better understand and relate to one another, to build greater bonds of communication, and to dive into deeper dialogues, then, HELL NO it isn't easier; smart phones do quite the opposite. Smart phones are good for telling someone you're running five minutes late, to check in for a flight, or to save some paper and use your GPS as opposed to printing directions (although, as you'll read in chapter 35, GPS is killing the world as well). Smart phones make our lives more complicated when people abuse/take for granted their functionality (which happens 99.99999 percent of the time).

- *Why is it that people have totally taken for granted how technologically amazing these devices are considering where they have come from in the past 20 years?* Because it is natural human instinct to take things for granted. For example, I have worked in the utility industry for the past several years. In this time, I feel like I have worked for two pretty good and fun organizations with lots of smart, hardworking people. However, 99 percent of the time that we get recognized in the community or in the press is when we mess up. If we keep people's lights on without fail for three consecutive years, we are given no praise because, despite the complexities of the energy business, people just expect that when they flip a light switch, the lights will come on; that is the way it has always been throughout their entire lives. Despite the fact that smart phones have existed for only a few years, we have already become accustomed to these technologies and very much take for granted how incredibly innovative they are despite the fact that most residences and businesses didn't even have the Internet (or a computer in general) only 20 years ago. (I know I made this point a few times; it is important to remember.) Now, almost everyone (besides my grandmother) has a smart phone.

- *What's next?* We all know what's next. Steve Jobs might not have been the first person to create a tablet, but he is the one who developed the marketplace for them. Within a year after the successful launch of the iPad, at least a dozen companies introduced to the marketplace what seemed to be 100 new tablets. Though most have not had the success of the iPad, the market for tablets is strong and only getting stronger. Will the tablet make the computer completely obsolete at some point in time? Perhaps. There certainly are limitations to where and when you can use a computer (including a laptop). Are we there yet? Not quite, but don't count out the idea. Essentially, what it would mean for all of us is that there would be another piece of mobile technology heavily engrained in our lives at all times of the day that serves to be as much as a distraction in our lives as anything else.

- *Should we say good-bye to natural human interaction altogether?* Stop being such a pessimist! (That's my job.) I'm going to continue fighting the good fight for all of us (kind of, but not really)!

- *Am I a hypocrite?* Yes, but it's not my fault. When my phone eventually died in October 2012, I was forced to buy a smart phone. I say I was forced because it felt like that; my brother stole my free upgrade, which meant if I wanted to get a new flip phone at that juncture, it would have cost me as much as a Samsung Galaxy S3. I knew the day would eventually come when I would be forced to cave, but I tried hard to hold my ground. In fact, the previous time I looked at new phones (around Sept 2011), I asked the attendant at the Verizon store if they had any flip phones for me to see. He laughed hard at me and told me that he thought they might have one or two models buried somewhere in the back room. Oh well. At least I tried to stay true to myself.

Several months after completing this chapter, I read an article in an issue of Businessweek *titled "The First Five Years of Mass Obsession." The article primarily discussed the impact of the iPhone through its first five years (aptly named article I suppose). The article contained a few interesting study results that I believe make a stronger case for many of my theories about how technology is consuming our lives and that I am right and everyone else is wrong. They include (and I quote):*

- *According to a study of medical workers at the Baystate Medical Center in Springfield, Mass., 76 percent say they've experienced "phantom vibration," that insistent buzz from an imagined text or phone call. Scientists speculate it's the result of random nerves firing, biochemical noise that our brains easily tuned out until they were reconditioned by the iPhone.*

- *"The iPhone has changed everything about how we relate to technology, for both good and bad," says Larry Rosen, a psychologist, professor, and author of* iDisorder: Understanding Our Obsession with Technology and Overcoming Its Hold on Us. *According to his research, nearly 30 percent of people born after 1980 feel anxious if they can't check* **Facebook** *every few minutes. Others repeatedly pat their pockets to make sure their smartphone [sic] is still there. Indulging those tiny, persistent urges brings us only a brief respite. "The relief is not pleasure," says Rosen. "That's the sign of an obsession."*

There are two final points I'd like to make based on these quotes: (1) I'd like to reiterate the "I'm right, you're wrong" point, and (2) it is a good thing you bought my book over Larry Rosen's because the title of his alone sounds pretty boring!

TEN

Turn Down The Bass! I Said, Turn Down The Fu—Nevermind!

Portable devices, like smart phones, have not only become a GREAT source of communication, they have also become a greater pain in my ass, especially when some dumbass wants everyone else around them to hear whatever it is they are listening to! But it's not only the portable devices that drive me insane ...

One of the greatest disruptions to the flow of natural human communication (and natural anything) that is hardly ever spoken about is bass as it is used on stereos, MP3 players, and such. I have never understood why people find it necessary to turn bass on any stereo or portable music listening device to the maximum levels, but then again, I am not the type of person that likes to feel like my heart or my eardrums are going to explode every time I hear a beat. Feel free to call me strange (if not for this reason then for others), but I actually like and appreciate my ability to function. I enjoy being able to hear a person I am in a conversation with at any given time because I am not temporarily (or permanently) deaf as a result of listening to music. At this stage in my life, I like all (most ... some) the people with whom I interact. That's not to say that later on in life when I am bitter, conservative, and stuck in my ways, I won't appreciate the deafness (or *selective hearing*) that comes with old age. But, for now, I am open to all (a few) thoughts, ideas, and interactions.

One of my greatest pet peeves is when someone in a fairly confined public setting (e.g., a bus) decides they want to make their ears bleed. This person turns up the volume on their iPod as loud as possible and makes sure to do the same with the bass. Now, this is wonderful for them, but for the other 40-60 people on the crowded bus ... well, they would rather worry just about themselves than having to listen to some loud, obnoxious noise that sounds like you've crawled inside a migraine. (For those of you who have never suffered a migraine, it feels like a jackhammer going off inside your head.)

I personally hate the completely selfish aforementioned actions to the point that I have decided to stand up to the madness; I am taking my listening arena back! Now, you may ask me, "How do you plan to do this? Will you use violence? If so, what will be your weapon of choice? A baseball bat (too easy)? A pitch fork (too sharp)? A grenade (too messy)?" Well, sirs and madams, if you have come to the conclusion that I am a violent person, we got this relationship off on the wrong foot. I am way more conniving than that. Plus, I don't want to do anything that could lead to prison time. I may be tall, but I am just too scrawny to survive in prison.

Though I am not violent, I have come up with steps to eradicate the bass-bumping situation most of the time (sometimes ... not often):

Step 1: The Death Stare
It is exactly what it sounds like. I stare at you with absolute focus and intent to the point that I am playing with your emotions and you are scared—you pretty much fear for your life. I am in your head and you want me out!

THE DEATH OF HUMAN INTERACTION

Step 2: The Deeper Death Stare

If the normal death stare fails me, I take it to a new level. I stare you down until my eyes bulge from my head. I have never reached this point, but I am a very committed individual; reaching the point where my eyes literally pop out of my eye sockets and fall to the ground is not out of the realm of possibility. I know you're thinking, "You would sacrifice your eyes for your ears?" This is a valid concern. However, as my wife will tell you, I am not much of a planner; I am more of a fly-by-the-seat-of-my-pants kind of guy. This means I will cross the eye-issue bridge when I come to it. Plus, if I lose my eyes, that's even more reason to get a (guide) dog, which I have wanted to get for years now.

Step 3: Polite Conversation

If steps 1 and 2 fail miserably (often the case), I will use my gentle, polite, nonthreatening nature as a weapon. In fact, I used this approach the other day on a person sitting directly next to me on the bus. This step basically entails starting a conversation with that person in hopes of making them feel bad about imposing upon my audio arena. In my encounter the other day, after the death stares failed, I tapped the shoulder of the guy sitting next to me. I asked him questions that I didn't really care about: "What are you listening to?" (As if I couldn't tell—the whole bus knew it was Ke$ha.) "What type of music do you like to listen to?" (Shitty! You like to listen to shitty music!!) "Do your ears ever hurt from listening to music so loud?" (You killed your hearing so long ago that you don't even realize you are listening to music anymore. At this point it is simply a style thing. In fact, I'm not entirely sure you can hear the words I am speaking to you.) To which he responded, "Ke$ha." (Nailed it!) "I don't know—just about anything." (See, I told you. No taste equals shitty taste in music.) "I don't even notice anymore; that's just the way I listen to it." Well, bud, that's great for you but have some common courtesy for the other people on the bus. (I suggest you take the Panzer's Personnel Etiquette and Self-Awareness for Jackasses 201, the follow-on class to 101, which will be focused on text-messaging etiquette.) After all, you don't want to push anyone riding the bus to and from work five days a week, who works long hours at a job that he absolutely loathes and is now looking for any reason to snap, to the brink of lewd behavior. (Not that I fit that description—I actually like my job). Which leads me to my next step …

Step 4: Put That Bastard in His/Her Place!

If steps 1 through 3 don't work, it is time to snap! Let loose and don't stop till the person flees, you run out of oxygen, or the cops show up and throw you in jail with some Occupy Wall Street protestors that just got teargassed. If you reach this step, you do want to keep your composure long enough to make sure you are closer to an exit than the person you are about to persecute and that you are quicker than them in case they trained in various forms of martial arts or happen to carry a gun. (WARNING: Only go to this step in extreme scenarios, like when someone is blasting the bass on either the formerly famous pop group Hanson or some gangsta rap, which, as I recall, died off about a decade ago.) However, more often than not, the person you yell at won't be able to hear you or understand what you're saying since they already destroyed their ability to hear long ago.

I can't escape it at home either (except when it is cold outside) …

During my first year and a half living in San Francisco, I resided in a neighborhood with a number of curious characters. My neighborhood was a bit rough to say the least (the projects were literally across the street from my front door), but I had to make that sacrifice in order to pay very reasonable rent (in San Francisco terms). Living there, I got to meet all sorts of interesting folks, like the 15 people that generally sat on my front porch on a sunny (or mildly overcast or any type of) day that were smoking blunts and drinking brown-bagged 40s. (I got to engage on a daily basis with the lady who used crates for a bed right in front of my neighbor's garage every afternoon. Every time she saw me she greeted me with a "Hi, Baby!" in a voice 15 times raspier than Marge Simpson.) Every night, 30 people gathered across

THE DEATH OF HUMAN INTERACTION

the street around a small table watching a few people play something. (It took me three months to realize they were playing dominos.)

However, the fun always started a little later at night when a whole bunch of cars with tinted windows rolled out onto the street and started blasting their bass on their car radios. (Thanks again, Galvin brothers!) It didn't matter if it was 7 p.m. or 1 a.m. (many of them didn't work a normal 9-5 day anyway); as long as it was dark and (oddly enough) somewhere between very warm and hot outside, they were bumping it hard. (It would be interesting to set up a sociological experiment to determine at what levels of darkness and at what temperature my neighbors would decide to blast their bass and, inversely, what temperature causes them to shut it down or never start to begin with.)

I used to always hope for warmer days during the summer months but not during my first year and a half in San Francisco. You see, when I say they would bump the music till all hours of the night, that means any day of the week; the neighbors across the street didn't discriminate between Wednesdays and Saturdays. When I first moved to the neighborhood and I would hear the bass going at 1 a.m., I would ask myself, "Do any of these people have jobs? If they do, don't they have to wake up in the morning?" After a few months, I realized that those were not the appropriate questions to ask. The best question to ask was, "WHEN THE FUCK IS IT GOING TO GET COLD?"

But during those days, since I greatly looked forward to getting at least a few hours of sleep on a daily basis to be awake and aware at work the next day (as I mentioned above, I like my job), I finally caved in and started calling the cops to file noise complaints. Trust me—I know what you're thinking. I also never thought I would become that person peeking through the blinds on my windows and gazing at those loud kids (although half of them were older than me) across the street who were being too loud as I used my other hand to dial the police. I used to make fun of those people all the time. However, calling the police seemed like a better solution than accepting the insomnia—which can make you less attentive and repetitive—that was being imposed upon me.

All I really want to know are the answers to the two following questions: (1) Is there anything wrong with listening to music at reasonable levels without blasting the bass? (2) Don't you realize that bass drowns out the best parts of almost every song?

Despite my obvious anger toward loud music/bass and the people that operate it, I shouldn't be overly critical. After all, as opposed to most chapters in this book where I describe how technology serves as a divide between two or more people looking to communicate with one another, the examples I used in this chapter ultimately led me to in-person conversations with a stranger on the bus and my neighbors. That being said, I don't think those people could hear what I was saying anyway, and if they could, I don't think they gave a rat's ass.

ELEVEN

Lesbians At The Pool

This is a rare occurrence for this book; I actually documented a story (well, more a point that solidifies the overarching message of my book) that happened during a business trip to Palm Springs. Enjoy ...

I flew to Palm Springs from San Francisco for several meetings over a two-day period. Day one had been an incredibly long day filled with travel, meetings, and ridiculously hot summer weather that peaked at over 110 degrees. So, what do you do after a long day when you arrive at your hotel in Palm Springs at 5 p.m. and it is still 109 degrees outside? You go to the pool.

That afternoon happened to be a rather quiet one at the pool. It was a Wednesday and schools had just started again, so hardly anyone was around. I was in a strong, serious relationship at the time (with the woman who is now my wife), so I was not looking for any kind of romance. However, I am what my friends call a "social butterfly," so I looked for some interesting conversation. As I looked around the pool I saw two groups of people. Group 1 was four European men, all wearing thongs and no shirts. Group 2 was a couple of cute girls that looked very approachable. Guess which group I chose to approach ...

You're wrong; I approached Group 2.

Sparking a conversation was easier than I imagined. I thought I would have to say something witty and feared being able to come up with anything given that my brain was mush from the day I spent in Dante's Inferno. Instead, I swam over to the corner of the pool near where they were lounging, and it didn't take long before they yelled out something corny to me: "Great music, huh?" (It wasn't (a) a good joke, or (b) good music.)

As we got to talking, I realized it was incredibly difficult to have a fluid conversation. I would say something to move the conversation in a new direction; for example, "I like sports" (a real brain stimulator). Then, the girl I was speaking to would quickly turn to her phone to send a text message or make a phone call. In the first five minutes of conversation, the only interesting detail I heard was that the one girl was a blackjack dealer at a local casino.

Because, as I mentioned, I was looking for "interesting conversation" and had never met a blackjack dealer outside a casino, I began going through my typical repertoire of endless questions. I quickly learned all sorts of rousing tidbits—don't hit on 13 when the dealer is showing a 6, don't double down when the dealer is showing a queen, and when you are dealt an ace and a jack, that makes blackjack and you automatically win. (You know, stuff that takes either years of experience or a genius to comprehend.) All would have been worthless and I would have moved on from the conversation had I not overheard one interesting conversation piece.

As we were *unfortunately* coming to a close on our blackjack conversation, I heard the one girl say to the other girl something along the lines of, "I don't think we're going to find any pussy at this pool tonight." (Yes, Mom. I agree that "pussy" is a dirty word, but I am using it in a quote.) HOLD THE PHONE ... Lesbians? I thought to myself, "Did I hear that correctly?"

THE DEATH OF HUMAN INTERACTION

I needed to find out if I heard that correctly. I have had numerous lesbian friends through the years, some of whom I am incredibly close with but none that I'd consider myself as attracted to as I was these two. Plus, as we all know, it is way easier to ask tough questions of complete strangers than people you care a good deal about and wouldn't want to offend. So, if they were in fact lesbians, this could be a great opportunity to answer some questions I've never been brave enough to ask. Consequently, I led the conversation toward the topic of homosexuality. The blackjack dealer quickly informed me that Palm Springs is like a "mini version of San Francisco—very gay." That explained other questions I had about Group 1, the European Speedo gang. Now it was time to cut right to the chase. I asked the blackjack dealer, "Are you gay?" She promptly answered "Yes." LESBIANS!

It was now time to take this conversation to the next level. As I did, the other girl started calling various girls to organize her all-women softball team. (I realize this sounds skeptically too stereotypical, but she really did.)

Me: I have a few questions for you that I hope you don't find offensive; if you find them to be too personal, please just tell me to shut the hell up. (My mother always taught me to be polite, even in absurd situations.)

Blackjack Dealer: I'm like an open book; fire away.

[Then, she quickly started texting on her iPhone again.]

Me: Well, you know how heterosexual men have penises, and they, well, stick them in the vaginas of women?

Blackjack Dealer: Yes.

[The blackjack dealer looked up for a moment then quickly refocused on her phone again.]

Me: And how homosexual men, who also have penises, stick them in orifices of other men for the sake of sexual stimulation?

Blackjack Dealer: Yes.

[The blackjack dealer is only half paying attention as I am teetering on the edge of a breakthrough as relevant as the creation of cold fusion.]

Me: What do homosexual women do in the bedroom with one another? I mean, I have a few guesses, but, well, ummm ...

Blackjack Dealer: Well, you know ... stuff.

"WELL, YOU KNOW ... STUFF?" WHAT THE FUCK? NO. NO. I was not going to let her settle there. I wanted to learn everything there is to know about scissoring. Is it mythology or reality? I was working on an interview the caliber of Frost-Nixon. I was the young, eager journalist with charisma and substantial nervousness flowing through my veins, and the blackjack dealer was an old, decrepit, former President that was calm in the moment, not realizing he was on the verge of cracking, providing the truth that millions of viewers (countless male readers) and I want to know.

Me: What do you mean by "stuff"?

Blackjack Dealer: Well, you know ...

No, I don't know. That is why I am asking you these questions, dammit! You have the goods. I want them. Now share!

Me: Well, does your sexual intercourse always involve toys?

Blackjack Dealer: Not necessarily.

THE DEATH OF HUMAN INTERACTION

I think, "You're going to have to do better than that for me!" But she dives back onto her phone. (Screw you, Apple! Well, I don't blame just Apple. If they hadn't created the iPhone, someone else would have. Although someone has to take the blame ... so, like I was saying, screw you, Apple!

Me: Not necessarily? Please elaborate.

Blackjack Dealer: You know ... I have slept with lots of guys before. I just haven't in a long time and prefer women.

Finally, she had shot a conversation starter my way. Unfortunately, she completely sidestepped the important question I had asked. But I agreed to move off this tangent, assuming we'd get back to the important topic in due time.

Me: So you are bisexual?

Blackjack Dealer: I don't know if I'd give myself that label.

Me: But you just said that you sleep with both women and men?

Blackjack Dealer: Uh huh.

Me: Isn't that the definition of bisexual?

Blackjack Dealer: I guess it is.

Her phone rang and she immediately answered it, leaving me wondering, "Is it a girl? Is it another cute lesbian? If so, are they going to make out tonight?" I started to get really excited. "Are they going to have sex tonight? Wait a second ... What are they going to do in the bedroom?" NOOOOOOOO!

My frustration kicked into high gear. I realized she never cleared up the uncertainty looming in my brain. Now she and her lesbian friend sitting next to her were both on their respective cell phones. Whoever said technology helps bring people closer together? At that moment, I couldn't have felt farther apart from the people sitting not even five feet away from me with whom I had been having a conversation for the past 45 minutes.

At that point, I conceded. (Yes, my male friends, I too am disappointed that I failed to learn the secrets of the female trade on this day. Perhaps one day I will be fortunate enough to uncover the mysteries and reveal them in a book dedicated entirely to this topic.) I got out of the pool, which after 45 minutes had dropped my internal temperature by 30 degrees, and moved into the hot tub to warm up a bit (in 108 degree weather).

As I sat there in the hot tub, I pondered what had just happened. The smart phone just killed what could have been one of the more enlightening conversations of my entire life. Would I ever be bold enough again to ask those difficult questions? (Probably, but when?) I looked over at Group 2 one last time and shook my head at the two of them, friends sitting side by side on a beautiful, sunny day, relaxing by the pool, both having conversations with someone on the other end of the phone that was miles away. I thought to myself, "Whatever happened to living in the moment?" Then I turned, looked at Group 1, and saw all four men crowded around one of their smart phones watching a video.

When did we reach the point in human history that the things in front of us became so lame that we have to extract entertainment from far-off places using our smart phones at all given times of the day? It is just another example of *The Death of Human Interaction*. (Someone please tell me it's not true!)

As I finished drafting this chapter, my wife called me, and as always, looked to learn about my day's events and find out what I was currently doing. I told her I was writing about one of the experiences from the day that would be a perfect story for this book. She, being a real-life on-camera journalist, inquired

THE DEATH OF HUMAN INTERACTION

further. I started to dive into the story about the lesbians but hesitated to tell her the types of questions I asked them. But she pried. I am weak, so I caved. I can't give more details about the remainder of the conversation because she would kick my ass for including a detailed conversation with her in this book. (Yes, I am afraid of her.) What I can tell you is she did use the phrase "muff-diving." Never thought I'd hear her say that.

By the way, the conversation between my wife and me took place over the phone, but it was in the privacy of my hotel room later on at night. It was not an interruption of a conversation I was having with someone regarding a topic in which they were incredibly interested. (But let's be honest ... those types of conversations don't happen very often because I am not all that interesting.)

TWELVE

Tech Geeks Have Won

My experience with lesbians may have ended anticlimactically (pun intended), but was it really their fault? Kind of. However, I gave them some benefit of the doubt. After all, that blackjack dealer and her friend did not invent the technology. The lesbians were simply unsuspecting pawns in a much bigger game of chess. There are much more malicious, disrespecting bastards out there (sort of) ...

At some point in life, everyone comes to a crossroads and asks themselves the age-old question, "What type of communicator am I?" (This assumes that you even know how to communicate with yourself and you actually give a rat's ass how people perceive you and your messages.) Are you a "face-to-face" type of person, the kind that likes to see the emotion and the body language of another person? Or are you an "I'm pretty shy and need some sort of medium in order to communicate with my fellow human being" type of person? I suppose what I am getting at is, are you a traditional or new-age communicator?

If you polled 100 people 50 years ago on this simple question, I am certain that the vast majority would align with the former; after all, we didn't have cell phones, most people didn't own a personal computer, there was no Internet, and there sure as hell was no Facebook.

If people wanted to communicate with one other, oftentimes they had to have a legitimate conversation.

In this day and age, however, the traditional communicators are sadly a dying breed. The infusion of a high volume of life-altering technologies—many of which are communication devices, programs, or systems—has changed the world. Instead of HAVING TO meet in person, you can take care of what you need to via e-mail. Instead of HAVING TO talk over the phone to make plans, you can text. Instead of HAVING TO talk with someone in order to get to know them, all you have to do is look at their Facebook page or LinkedIn page or Match.com page or do a Google search on them. People no longer HAVE TO or NEED TO incorporate the soft attributes of communication in their lives; instead, they can cut right to the details. What fun is that? And, more importantly, how did we get here?

Well, in any time of change, we get from point A to point B by following the footsteps of our leaders. In this case, our leaders have been Technology Geeks (Tech Geeks). They are not the heroic leaders of the past like Julius Caesar or William Wallace or George Washington (hell, none of the Tech Geeks probably know how to ride a steed or handle a weapon), but they are the visionaries that have captured our attention and imaginations (and souls). Tech Geeks have dreamt ways to improve upon our world and our society and sold us in the process. Now it is my turn to open your minds to a whole new theory based on one simple reality … Tech Geeks are entirely (for the most part) the most antisocial, noncommunicative people in the world.

Tech Geeks turned the world we all once knew upside down because they realized they were at the bottom of the hierarchical social food chain; instead of becoming better communicators themselves, they decided to bring the rest of us down. Think about it for just one moment. Did the population of the world survive for thousands of years before Martin Cooper introduced the cell phone? Did people have a means of attaining information before the creation of

THE DEATH OF HUMAN INTERACTION

the Internet? Did people have the capability to make new friends and build upon existing friendships before the introduction of Facebook? Of course they did!

Now ask yourself, who is best served by a website like Match.com, someone who has some attitude and flare that knows the right thing to say when he meets a girl at a bar or a Tech Geek who graduated from Yale with a degree in computer science and whose best-known icebreaker was the time he choked and almost died on Icebreaker gum while nervously approaching a woman? Who is making millions of dollars on new startups, like gaming apps for iPhones, and thus attracting supermodel girlfriends that simply want them for their *brains*? (Granted, their relationships are shallow, but 50 years ago, no Tech Geek in the world walked around with a 5-foot-11 blonde bombshell on his arm. They worked for NASA by day and hoped to not to go bald by night.)

If you used to be one of those "traditional" communicators, I hate to break it to you but you have been played. Unfortunately, I don't have any easy solutions for you on how to get the world back in order. All I can tell you is to shut your devices, systems, and programs down; shut all of them down. Throw your smart phone out the window. Erase your Facebook profile. Tear your GPS off your dashboard and smash it on the curb. Hit the power button on everything else and never look back. Oh, and pray that everyone else does the same; otherwise, you will be a fish out of water. (Hopefully no one gets hurt—except the Tech Geeks—by the devices being hurled out windows should people heed my advice.)

Truth be told, the technologies that consume our lives are here to stay; at this point they are so engrained in our lives that we blew by the point of no return ages ago. The Tech Geeks won, but don't feel sad. Be consoled by the realization that the rest of us lost together—or become a Tech Geek yourself and get that supermodel girlfriend!

THIRTEEN

Dial-Up To Wifi

The first major step those Tech Geeks took in pushing the social world online was introducing the Internet to households. Ironically, despite the fact that the first form (dial-up) of the Internet was the slowest, most aggravating method of communication, people were still drawn in and patient enough to wait for the connections that we have today that have led to the Death of Human Interaction. It's similar to someone strapping themselves into the electric chair and waiting for the generator to be built. Dying is fun! YAAAAAYYY!

A long, long time ago, between approximately two and fifteen years ago (ironically I don't presently have access to free wireless Internet to go onto Wikipedia to confirm the facts of this chapter as I happen to be sitting in the Oakland Airport), John Francis WiFi invented the aptly named WiFi function. Since then, the world has vastly changed ...

Dial-Up Internet

Way back in the day, most people relied on dial-up Internet, which, compared with today, is outrageously pitiful. You see (for people too young to remember and those with only short-term memory, which is pretty much everyone these days), in the early days of the World Wide Web (the "Internet" for those unfamiliar), the primary means of getting and being connected was by way of telephone lines. Typically, one would log on to a service like AOL or Prodigy by entering a username and password, clicking enter, and allowing the computer to dial a 1-800 number that connected them to a server. From there, people were able to check e-mail, instant message, go into chat rooms, and surf the Internet.

It was fantastic ... except for the fact that it was slower than shit. For example, there were times that I would try to sign off and I would watch as it slowly connected over a 15-minute period. Sometimes this was due to the fact that telephone lines were not the best means for this function, while other times it was due to a variety of reasons, from busy signals on the receiving end to a problem with the software. As a teenager who was super-pumped to get home from school and immediately start instant messaging via AOL with my friends I had just seen 20 minutes prior, this service was disheartening; however, I stuck with it as it was new, cool, and I had no other alternatives.

Despite the fact that dial-up was a pain in the ass, there were some advantages to it. For instance, if either of my brothers ever pissed me off, I could always get back at them by waiting until they signed on to AOL, go into a separate room, and pick up the phone until the dial-up connection disconnected. Alternatively, if they were on the phone, I could always try several times to log on to the Internet, making them hear the annoying dial-up sound time and time again until they lost their minds and their phone conversation was killed. (Being the youngest son, I had to come up with strategic attacks on my brothers because I was shorter than them until around 10th grade.)

Broadband Internet

Around the time that I started college, broadband Internet was the new thing; it was even cooler than the Backstreet Boys if you can imagine that. (For older generations reading this book, it was even cooler than the Osmonds.) And, conveniently enough, the residential

THE DEATH OF HUMAN INTERACTION

communities that seemed to get this capability earliest were colleges and universities. Hence, when I started my freshman year at Syracuse University, I said good-bye to slow, crappy dial-up and hello to high-speed, wonderful, magical broadband!

But it wasn't just the broadband that was so perfect. It was also a time of freedom (some that kids today will never understand). In the early part of the 2000s, people had the freedom to illegally download music via Napster (not that I ever would), watch Internet porn without signing our lives away that we were who we were and that we were 18 years of age or older (not that I ever did), and gamble online (I may have done this from time to time). For my generation, the early days of broadband Internet were comparable to the 1960s hippy days for my parents. It was all about peaceful nonconformity. (Unfortunately, that all changed as Internet regulations became more intense.) The only real constraint was that your computer physically had to be plugged in using an Ethernet cable in order to be able to access the Internet, which brings us to ...

Wireless Internet

In the middle part of the 2000s, the opportunity to access the Internet wirelessly quickly proved to be a reality. In practically no time, people began replacing their now-common broadband Internet with what the Australians (and all other English-speaking societies) called a "wireless router." As long as you had the appropriate technologies hooked up to or installed on your computer, you could explore the vast World Wide Web from anywhere that was close enough to the wireless router for you to receive a signal. The best part about this was obvious: You didn't have to deal with stupid, annoying, lame cords anymore. You could move all around your house, apartment, or mansion (I'll tell you more about what that is like in my next book—after this book sells one hundred million copies in hard cover) without serious concerns over logistics. It was pretty fly! However, there were still restrictions. For example, once someone left a building that had wireless

Internet and was on the go, they no longer had access to high-speed, high-quality Internet. John Francis WiFi knew this had to change!

WiFi

I have no idea how he did it. I have no idea why he did it. I have no idea how none of you have heard of John Francis WiFi, the inventor of WiFi.

When John Francis WiFi invented WiFi, I do think he understood the impact it would have on the world. WiFi has revolutionized the Internet in the sense that you can access it anywhere at any time. And it's fast too … as fast as any home wireless broadband connection (mostly). Think about where we have gone in the past 15 to 20 years. We started out with no Internet, went to slow (shitty) dial-up Internet, on to high-speed (wire-bound) broadband Internet, then to wireless (equally high-speed yet constrained) broadband Internet, and now to high-speed Internet EVERYWHERE! But is that a good thing?

Relying on my extensive (nonexistent … I took one course in college and it had no relevance to this topic) sociological training, I say no. All it means is that people have more opportunities to be dialed in to the online world and completely disconnected/removed from the real world. But, to be fair, it's not like people are wasting any less time on the Internet than back during the days of dial-up. The difference is that broadband, wireless, and now WiFi have simply made people more efficient at wasting their time—meaning they can do a lot more in the same amount of wasted time (and they are).

Only time will tell if John Francis WiFi's key contribution to the world was one of the greatest the world has ever known or just another step on the path of idiocracy and introverts. One thing we do know is that it has allowed text-based communication to become even more powerful.

FOURTEEN

Real-Time Direct Text-Based Chatting Communication (A.K.A. Instant Messanging)

Instant messaging has been a function in our lives for what seems like forever. It started through services like Prodigy and took off during the popularity peak of America Online. For the multitasker, it was wonderful, but it had (and still has) the potential to be detrimental to the naïve user that seemed to forget that computers have the ability to automatically save conversations.

Assuming I am correct, and I usually (hardly) am, I claim that the first major technological shift from my parents' generation to mine came with the creation of the instant message. (One might say the cell phone, but that is simply a mobilized version of technology that has been around for a hundred years.) The instant message (and all verbal forms of instantaneous communication to follow ... text messages, Twitter, etc.) introduced to the world a shift away from longer, more tedious forms of communication, such as in-person conversations (logistically tedious), e-mailed and/or snail-mailed letters (lengthy), and telephone conversations (lengthy and tedious)). With instant messaging, you could speak to dozens of people, holding several conversations about a number of different topics all at once. Almost overnight, the world shifted from thoughtful, focused, attentive conversations to ADD-style, very scatterbrained yet *efficient* conversations. Yes, in no time, you could find out what you missed in your poli sci class that you slept through earlier in the morning (from one friend) and if that girl you met at the bar last night is into you (through her friend that you happen to have on your instant message list), and you could make plans to play basketball in a couple hours (with a bunch of your friends). All these conversations could happen simultaneously.

The magical part that made all this work to perfection was the creation of a new (unofficial) language that supported the efficiency. The new language essentially took emotions and words from the English language and either pared them down or combined a whole bunch of words together. For example (and stop me if you've heard this one), should you want to go grab a beverage, take your laundry out of the washer, or take a dump, instead of typing "be right back" (although "be right back" in the last scenario would be an understatement for any guy), you could simply type "brb"—that says it all! Whomever you happened to be instant messaging would know they had to wait to continue (or end) the conversation until you came back. (And, admit it, there have often been times you have forgotten for hours to come back. When you finally did, you came back to a message reading "cya" or "ttyl" meaning "see you" or "talk to you later," respectively, and you inferred a pissed-off tone as you read it.) Obviously, "brb" is a classic, but my personal favorite has always been "lol," which stands for "laughing out loud." Instead of taking the time to acknowledge how funny someone is with a lengthy "hahahhaha-hahahhahahahahhahaa," all you have to type is "lol." What can be easier than that? And you don't even have to expend the energy actually laughing out loud.

Another bonus: the verbal communication we get to use in instant messaging doesn't have to be grammatically accurate either. It's a good thing I hardly paid attention in English class from eighth grade on. I woulda dun a hole lotta learnin' dat, woulda been useles 4 me after only a few moor years. Who needs good grammar anyway? Hell with

THE DEATH OF HUMAN INTERACTION

it! It's not like I will one day want to write a book that I hope other people will want to read and be able to follow via the use of proficient grammar (ooops …).

Beyond efficiency and good grammar (or the lack thereof), I think two great things to come out of instant messaging (especially during the early years of America Online) are (1) the cool screen names you got to assign yourself, and (2) the smiley faces.

Back in the AOL days, screen names were a source of identity. That is one of the lame things I will mention about g-chat (Google chat) and Facebook chat. In both, your instant messenger name is typically your name. Is there anything fun about that? Not really! If I wanted to be called Aaron Panzer, I would go talk to someone in person (which I clearly have no desire to do anymore now that I have all this cool technology at my disposal). With instant messaging, I want to have a cool name, like "ChatRouletteCreeper69" (please refer to chapter 15). I don't care if every other single person in the world (well, with the exception of about 99.9999999999999 percent of the people in the world) know that Aaron Panzer is ChatRouletteCreeper69; it makes me feel like I have an alter ego and that is fun.

For example, when I was a teenager, the cool thing to do was get an AOL account so that you could rush home from school and talk to everyone you had just seen ALL DAY LONG using (dial-up) instant messenger. (The days that the dial-up connection didn't work were absolutely crushing!)

We all had fun names, but I have to say that mine was definitely the coolest. I guarantee that there were not that many white kids growing up in a very non-diverse, suburban, middle-class community in this country that had a screen name as fly as (wait for it … a little longer … and … now) "ChilIn187." That's right, for all of you that have always wondered who was the lucky bastard to claim that stellar AOL name you all wanted, it was me, Aaron Panzer aka Chill-N-1-8-7!

(To be honest, I probably heard that phrase in a gangsta rap song at one point and it just stuck. It wasn't until a couple years later that I learned that "187" is slang often used in gangsta rap songs referring to the California Penal Code, Section 187 which defines the crime of murder.) That's right ... thug life! (Ironically, Notorious B.I.G., one of the musical names from the era of gangsta rap, died by way of a 187 in Los Angeles, California, on my 15th birthday, which totally justifies my having that screen name.)

About as far from thug life as you can get are smiley faces. Prior to instant messaging, I did not even realize the level of creativity that you could come up with using your keyboard alone as a tool for displaying your mood. Perhaps today I am feeling pretty happy, so I can type ":" followed by ")" (in that order) giving me the final product of ☺. Maybe it is raining outside, my girlfriend just dumped me, and I found out that I am going bald. I can type ":" followed by "(" to get ☹. Or maybe the person I am talking with over instant message is teasing me a lot and I decide to tease back. I could follow all the teasing action with ":" and then "P" to show :P, which makes it look like I am sticking my tongue out at you, almost to say, "In your face!" Aren't smiley faces the best? ☺☺

(Now I'm just bored with them and tired of typing.)

Protect yourself from the Tyler Willingham's of the world

Tyler (should you ever read this), I would have left you anonymous in this story, but you embarrassed me in front of 60 people that I know personally. I feel like it is fair for the few readers of this book to be warned about the malicious nature of your pranks. Hopefully, your significant other reads this, realizes what a dick you can be, and withholds sex for the next several months in punishment. Or your kids read this one day and pull a prank on you that is just as embarrassing.

THE DEATH OF HUMAN INTERACTION

For all of you reading this book that don't personally know me (all five readers of this book do know me), I would say that I can be a bit of a prankster once in a while (often), especially in the office environment. I generally get fairly bored if I am not scheming up a plan against a friend or coworker. I have pulled numerous pranks—from posting an ad for my friend's car on Craigslist at a very reasonable price (and included his telephone number in the ad), to rearranging a coworker's entire cube, to putting a flyer all over campus that included a picture of a graduate school classmate wearing a bib with a lobster picture on it while holding giant crab legs and suggesting he was on PETA's top 10 most wanted list. (I know they sound like stupid pranks, but in better context—knowing these people—they were very appropriate and at least mildly funny.)

Because of karma, every dumb prankster like me probably deserves a Tyler Willingham in their life (even though I never personally pulled a prank on him). And, in retrospect, I can honestly say it was a highly embarrassing, probably mean, but very funny prank.

Tyler and I were coworkers in my first job out of college at a multi-faceted entertainment company in Los Angeles. Tyler was a *big time* assistant to one of the partners, the head of the music management department, and I was a lowly (notice how I didn't use italics here ... because it was true) mailroom guy. (Sadly, my title was officially "Mailroom" although I preferred to think of myself as a college educated gopher.) On certain occasions, when one of the assistants was going to be out of the office for whatever reason, the other mailroom guy, one of the two receptionists, or I filled in at their desk. Being an assistant basically entailed doing all the lame logistical work for their boss. Fortunately for me, Tyler was a very anal bastard who was about five days ahead of schedule on all his work, so the one day I was asked to sit at his desk, I had plenty of time to take care of the important things on my plate, like winning at Minesweeper and instant messaging friends to make plans for that weekend.

While I was between instant messages with a couple friends and starting to get bored with it, a girl that I had previously dated a couple times decided to message me. This girl, as I recall, was the worst. She switched from very hot to very cold at the drop of a hat. One minute she was fun, vibrant, and appeared very into me; she seemed like the coolest girl around. The next minute, she came off as schizophrenic; she would claim that someone was out to get her and tell me to stay the hell away. The thing that kept me hanging around was that I was a 23-year-old guy with raging hormones and she was a hard 9.5 out of 10, physically speaking (probably 2 out of 10 when you mix in the crazy). Plus, every guy wants a crazy girl at some point in his life. (Even homosexual men want a crazy girl at some point in their lives just to have something juicy to talk about.)

If she had messaged me at the exact same time a week prior, I probably would have acted differently from what I am about to describe, but earlier in the week she displayed her looney side (essentially she threw herself at me then immediately told me I had to leave and leave now); I was starting to get fed up with her. So, I decided to toy with her a bit in my messaging that day. I told her stuff like, "I can't stop thinking about you. You are the girl of my dreams. I ache for you. Please don't leave me. I want you so badly. Let's make love for the first time in a rose garden. Any chance I can get a blumpkin?" (To be honest, I don't really remember what I wrote. I only remember that it was lame, childishly deceitful, and absurd. Again, I was 23 years old with raging hormones and this girl was driving me mad.)

There is a small part of me that feels bad about toying with someone in a conversation to the level that I did with her that day. A much greater part of me feels foolish that I copied the entire conversation into an e-mail (again, while using Tyler's computer), sent the conversation to my roommate (as he was familiar with my situation with this girl and I thought he might get a laugh), and forgot to erase the e-mail from Tyler's "sent" box. I don't know when, but at some point

THE DEATH OF HUMAN INTERACTION

between that day and two months later when I decided to leave the company, Tyler found the e-mail with the conversation I had with that girl.

As I have done on every job that I have left, I prepared and sent out a good-bye letter to the people I worked with, thanking them for the good times, the experience, the friendship, and the support. In return, I expected that I might get a couple e-mails from some of my coworkers wishing me well, which did happen. What I didn't expect was that Tyler was going to "reply to all" with a doctored up version of my instant message conversation that I had with that girl and had subsequently sent to my roommate. To his credit, Tyler did not add any language to the conversation; however, he did remove a fair amount of language that, in the end, made me appear to be madly in love with this girl, desperately pleading for her to give me a chance to show her that she was in love with me too. Given that this was a 60-person company and Tyler wanted his audience to be as big as he could get, his response went out to everyone, including the five partners who managed entertainers such as Jim Carrey, Will Ferrell, Ellen DeGeneres, Bette Midler, Vince Vaughn, Green Day, and The Goo Goo Dolls; the producer of such movies as *Batman Begins*, *The Dark Knight*, and *12 Monkeys*; and the head of Dick Clark Productions.

I spent the first half hour after reading Tyler's e-mail hiding in a stuffy video closet away from everyone and everything; I was thoroughly embarrassed. Subsequent to that first half hour, once the shock wore off, I decided to embrace the situation. After all, I was the one who did (perhaps cruelly) mess with that (possibly psychologically challenged) girl over instant messenger. And, throughout my year at the company, I did often pull numerous pranks on people; I probably got what I deserved. Also, it was a very funny, well executed prank; I couldn't be mad about that. It also didn't hurt that Tyler was fired from the company for his actions the very next day. (No, he wasn't ... another lie.)

A few lessons I learned from this experience include:
1. Karma is a bitch. Just smile when it slaps back.
2. Don't trust Tyler Willingham—ever! In fact, to be safe, don't trust anyone named "Tyler."
3. Everything you write or type in an instant message, text message, e-mail, tweet, etc. is traceable. Clean up your paper trail (if that's even possible these days)!

In all seriousness, if you need one more reason to go back to conversing with others in person, this story serves as a reminder that written or typed messages can be misinterpreted, misrepresented, or altogether altered (by the Tyler Willinghams of the world). If you want to deliver a clear message (and don't want the stress of worrying whether or not your message will come back to bite you in the ass later on), go talk to someone face-to-face. If my conversation with that girl had been face-to-face, I probably never would have fucked with her. (I wouldn't have had the balls too—she was a certifiable, crazy bitch.) I certainly never would have sent an e-mail to my roommate with the entire transcript of the conversation, and I never would have had to hide in a video closet on my last day of work at my first job out of college.

Once upon a time, a letter, written using a pen and paper, was the only form of written communication. Because it took more time, required accuracy on the first go (you can't erase ink), and made your hand sore after too much of it, people had to be more thoughtful in what they wrote and what they didn't. With electronic communication, written text is easier, potentially endless, and not discreet; that leads to more miscommunications and more mistakes (like drunken texts ... we've all had those).

Seriously, stop with the texting, stop with the instant messaging, stop with the electronic written communication; otherwise, you will encounter your own Tyler Willingham one day and he may be more of a dick than mine. Oh, and video chat isn't much better ...

FIFTEEN

Life Is A Game And So Is Chatroulette

If there is one thing worse than having a prank pulled on you in front of 60 of your colleagues, it's playing ChatRoulette and seeing a 55-year-old dick in your face broadcast from Russia!

In order to perform the proper research to write this chapter, I just used ChatRoulette for the very first (and only) time. I previously heard from many how ridiculous this service is (e.g., you are guaranteed to see genitals of some sort); I never imagined how stupid it actually is until now. Like most people, during my first (and, again, only) time, within four clicks, I saw a penis. No, no, I didn't. Seeing a penis would have been way cooler than anything I saw. (I realized after the fact that I never saw a penis because the default setting for me indicated that I did not want to see any nudity.)

For those of you that have never been on ChatRoulette, it is essentially a program that is incredibly simple to start using. Once you log on to the website, you can immediately start clicking from video chat to video chat. You actually don't even need to have a camera and/or microphone set up on your computer to participate. (I have both but luckily could not get them working; no one will ever know that I spent some time on ChatRoulette—with the exception of the five people that read this book ... thanks again Mom, Dad, Jeff, Marc, and Katie.)

ChatRoulette links you to other people playing with this website from all over the world. Within three clicks, I went from getting a live feed from a guy in Turkey to a guy in the U.S. to a guy in China to a guy in Russia. (Did not you notice how many times I said "guy"?) I clicked again and there was a guy from South Africa on the screen. Clicked again and there was a guy from Italy on the screen. One more click and I saw a male neighbor from the land of the Canucks. One more click and I saw two girls from the States. One more click and I saw a cat on a futon in Uzbekistan. (Who even knew they had futons there and that they keep cats as domestic animals?) Then, the next few clicks ... all guys again!

My little research experiment led me to the simple conclusions that 99 percent of people and 95 percent of all users (apparently domestic animals enjoy getting in on the game) that use ChatRoulette are lonely, horny, bored guys that turned that "no nudity" setting off. Guys, here are a couple simple thoughts:

1. This is no way to spend each one of your birthdays from age 14 to 86. (Those 87 years old and older are not very tech savvy ... not yet at least.)
2. Go to a park, go to a Starbucks, go hop on a bus (but don't sit next to someone who is blasting their bass ... refer to chapter 10), and meet some people. Ask a girl (or a guy) out on a date. If things work out well (enough), you'll get to see some genitalia in person, and that is much better than through a computer screen!
3. Skype nudity/sex is way more intimate (or so I've heard ... my wife won't let me try it when I am out of town for work).

Speaking of Skype ...

SIXTEEN

Skype: Chatroulette Might Be Less Awkward

One form of communication that (kind of) helps ease the pain of being away from your loved ones is Video Chat. Skype, the company that seemed to truly make it popular and available, would probably say their service helps us keep and maintain stronger connections with one another. I would say it can make a Jewish mom happy (particularly mine) and drive a Jewish son mad (particularly me) ...

My first introduction to Skype came during the fall of 2008 when I was studying abroad in Copenhagen as part of a graduate school exchange program. Due to the international separation, the outrageous cost of phone charges, and the fact that Skype is an easy (and free) software to use, my mother thought Skype would be an excellent way for my parents and me to stay connected during my few months away. I protested time and time again, making excuse after excuse, exclaiming that I had no microphone or camera on my computer; hence, I physically lacked the capabilities to use Skype.

(When I am abroad, I realize I have a limited amount of time to explore the country and immerse myself in the history and culture of wherever I happen to be at that given time. I try not to distract myself with life back home because it will still be there when I get back. I feel like if I don't do as much with my time as I can, then I shortchange myself because that particular adventure is probably only coming around once. To put it lightly, Lori Panzer does not see eye to eye with me on this one.)

However, like most Jewish mothers would and regardless of how I felt about it, my mother remedied my technological situation; she sent me a camera with a microphone to plug into my computer. I was trapped; I was out of excuses! (In retrospect, I suppose I could have lied and told her that the camera was destroyed in shipping, even though she secured it between five rolls of toilet paper.)

On an almost daily basis, my mother would shoot me an e-mail or an instant message telling me to sign onto Skype real quick because she had *one* thing she had to tell me. (My mother is known for always having *one* thing or *one more* thing to tell me or my brothers. I could be immersed in flames, screaming into the phone in utter agony telling her I must immediately dive into a body of water before my skin melts off completely, and she would respond by saying, "Just *one* more thing ....") In her life, my mother never had only *one* thing to say, and even if she did, it almost never required an immediate conversation. Truth be told, my mother loves me very much, and I love her (that's part of the reason I give her such a hard time). But she is batshit crazy and can be very needy (especially of her third and youngest child). So, throughout my time in Copenhagen, we Skyped ...

The Skypes between my mother and me usually occurred at nighttime in Copenhagen and morning time in San Diego. She would ALWAYS comment on how dark it was behind me in Copenhagen. (It was, after all, nighttime in the fall and winter in a city that sits at the same latitude as northern Canada and southern Alaska ... so no shit—it was dark!) She would ALWAYS comment on how I hadn't shaved again (and I wouldn't because I didn't have a job to go to—one of the beauties of graduate school). She would ALWAYS comment on the fact that I seemed to wear the same hoodie. (I am a creature of habit, and none

THE DEATH OF HUMAN INTERACTION

of you can change me ... I dare you to try!) Then she would tell me that the dog missed me and that "Dad is a dork," but he wanted to say "hello." Then my dad would appear in front of the screen and say something along the lines of "There's my dude!" or "Are you meeting lots of Swedes?" (He didn't ask the latter to be sarcastic. He just ... can be a space cadet from time to time. Dad, I love you too!) This was the same exact conversation we had on an almost daily basis for five months!

Honestly, even though having the same conversation in the same exact fashion for months on end was a bit exhausting, that was never the worst part. The worst part was the actual video portion. I realize that while I was growing up, the notion of videophones was often discussed in a "the future of telecommunications is coming" sort of way. Videophones were going to be a device that changed the way families and friends stayed in touch, even with great distances separating them. Not only could you talk to a person over the phone, you could actually see them while doing it (FAN-FREAKIN-TASTIC!). It was going to be real *neat-o*!

Well, I'd like to inform 12-year-old Aaron that video chatting is not nearly as *neat-o* as we all envisioned. It is actually quite awkward because you are essentially staring at the person you are talking with in an intense fashion. On one hand, you feel obligated to stare at the person you are talking with because if you don't, you feel like you are being rude or they think you are ignoring them; in which case, you might as well not even be Skyping with them because they are not in same place as you. You might as well just have a phone conversation instead. On the other hand, it is very unnatural to stare at someone during an entire in-person conversation for 15 minutes, 30 minutes, or an hour, and it doesn't feel any less natural to do it on a computer screen. In most in-person conversations (at least the ones I'm involved in), people generally look in many different directions throughout; if you stare at the person without looking around at all, it feels uncomfortable and weird for both parties involved.

On top of the uncomfortable feelings video chatting brings, it creates one other problem for me. Surprisingly, though I was once in a long-distance relationship, I rarely ever Skyped. In fact, I would Skype only on the rare occasion that I reached the point of maximum frustration with the terrible cell phone reception in my home. Typically, I prefer to chat over the phone (although that can feel like a burden from time to time). I feel like, for the most part, when speaking over the phone, I can hold a pretty solid conversation and multitask at the same time. (My ex-girlfriend with whom I was in a long-distance relationship would beg to differ.) Either way, when she called me out on multitasking or not listening intently, I would disagree and hold a firm ground. When we Skyped, I lost that ability entirely. The visual imagery projected from my computer to hers told a story with which I couldn't argue, and I love to argue!

Skype, you have stripped some good clean fun out of my life. And without the opportunity to multitask, you have made me a little less productive and efficient. Are you happy with yourself?

To be honest, simply seeing someone on the screen in a video chat is not what makes me uncomfortable; it's seeing someone I personally know. That is why ChatRoulette is way more fun and appealing—it's much less awkward if you don't know the person!

While I might not be the ideal customer for Skype, it does have a strong hold on the market amongst middle-aged Jewish mothers that like to keep tabs on their children.

SEVENTEEN

And On The Eighth Day,
God Invented *Friendster*

Everything I have discussed up to this point feels like nothing compared to the technologies outlined in chapters 17-24. You guessed it, social media technologies! All the hardware and software and infrastructure I debated in previous chapters are essentially the means of the Death of Human Interaction. Social media is the ends! (I hope I just made my college philosophy professor and Immanuel Kant proud!) And though it is tough to pinpoint the absolute first social media platform, you can make as good of a case for Friendster as anything.

Does anyone remember Friendster? For those that do remember, do you even care about Friendster anymore? In case you are one of the millions of people who never heard of it during the momentary blip in history when Friendster was relevant, it was, in some regard, the first major social networking site. It was a predecessor to a few small websites you may have heard of including Facebook, MySpace, and LinkedIn. And, though its name is hardly spoken anymore (except, surprisingly, in Asia—which I learned while traveling from village to village in search of my prepubescent love slave, Anwan Lau, whom I ultimately found on Friendster), it is still alive and kicking. Despite its lack of popularity today in the U.S., Friendster was once very hip.

Friendster was founded in 2002 by Jonathan Abrams and Ross MacKinnon (both computer programmers) when they alienated all their friends. The truth of how they did this has been heavily debated in several capacities throughout the past 10 years. One source claimed to have received e-mail chains from the two with a message stating that if he forwarded the e-mail to 50 of his closest friends within one hour, he would be rewarded with luck. The day after that source forwarded the e-mail, he was fired from his job, his wife left him, and his son finished the remaining Cinnamon Toast Crunch in the house—and he loved Cinnamon Toast Crunch.

Another source claimed that Abrams and MacKinnon, without realizing they were simultaneously pulling the exact same prank on one another, hacked into each another's AOL instant messenger accounts and wrote crude messages to every single one of their respective *buddies*. Regardless of what the truth really was, Jonny and Ross were desperate for friends. Hence, Friendster was born!

Abrams and MacKinnon claimed to have founded Friendster "to create a safer, more effective environment for meeting new people by browsing user profiles and connecting to friends, friends of friends, and so on, allowing members to expand their network of friends more rapidly than in real-life, face-to-face scenarios." (Of course, I took this quote directly from my favorite source, Wikipedia! For more details regarding my abuse of this fabulous resource, please check out chapter 36.) Oh, sorry ... I believe I omitted the final portion of that quote, "...and to waste their fucking time!" Yes, yes, yes! People love to waste their time social networking on the computer. And I (from a place of absolutely no authority) would like to proclaim Friendster as the first social networking website of its kind.

Friendster was truly an amazing breakthrough. It took something as exciting as Classmates.com to the next level. (All of you should know what Classmates.com is; after all, it has been advertised everywhere online for the past 15 years. It is that advertisement that tells you to check to see what all your old classmates from high school have been up to while displaying some random picture from a yearbook taken in the latter half of the 1960s.) Classmates.com was simple. All you had to do was sign up, create a profile, find your alma mater, and see who else had signed up. Then, if you actually wanted to connect or communicate with the people you never actually spoke to when you were two feet away from one another in the same classroom throughout four years of high school, all you had to do now was pay a small fee. What a solid proposition, right?

Unlike Classmates.com, Friendster was completely free—monetarily speaking. It took from you only your privacy, self-respect, and time—I think that might be all. Friendster also made it much easier to find your friends. You no longer had to limit yourself to searching only by school. Instead, you could search by name. Plus, most results that showed up from the search included a picture, which helped you to deduce that either you had indeed found the person you were searching for or you were on the wrong track.

I personally chose a picture of Jason Biggs, the actor from *American Pie*, for my profile picture because most people generally recognized me more often as Jason Biggs than Aaron Panzer. (Thanks to that movie, I have been asked more times than you can imagine, in several embarrassing scenarios, if I have either "fucked a pie" or "fingered a pie." The answer to those questions is a story for another time. I generally respond by saying, "3.14159265." That confuses them long enough for me to walk away.) Also, in case you didn't want to limit yourself to only former classmates from high school, you could track or be tracked down by friends, friends of friends, or random people you didn't even know (whom I like to call "stalkers" ... not that there are crazy people on the Internet).

Friendster was also the first website to establish the types of social networking dilemmas that exist today. For example, one day, when my brother Jeff first invited me to start my very own profile and become his *friend* on Friendster, I gladly accepted. Soon after, we were no longer just brothers; we became *friends* on Friendster. Then, my other brother, Marc, saw that I was *friends* with Jeff on Friendster as he was too. (On this magical program, you could see who your friend's friends were.) So Marc sent me an invitation to also become *friends*. While I thought about this invitation a few moments longer than I thought about Jeff's, I knew deep down in my heart that I would not regret being *friends* with my oldest brother. So I accepted him. Life on Friendster started out great! However, it was only just beginning; there was a lot of Friendster out there to experience, so I set out to do just that!

I realized it was time for me to search for new friends to build my profile. Some people are content with their family members being their only friends. I, however, am not one of them; I am a social butterfly, so I had to let my wings soar. I found person after person that I hadn't thought about or heard from in years, but now we had an opportunity to be reunited online ... through Friendster! Those first few hours of searching, I went on a shopping spree for old friends; in no time I sent 75-100 *friend* requests. Once everyone accepted, my life would be awesome! Within a few more hours, I would be more popular than both Marc and Jeff combined. Suck it, brothers! (Being the youngest brother, I may have built up a slightly competitive attitude throughout the years that may or may not be directed toward my brothers.)

Later that day, I logged back onto Friendster to see how many dozens of *friends* I now had—12! One dozen *friends*, including Marc and Jeff! I couldn't believe it. Only 10 other schmucks besides Marc and Jeff wanted to be *friends* with me on Friendster (which meant I had an acceptance rate of only about 10 percent ... WTF!). Don't get me wrong—I was happy to add those 10 other schmucks to my list, but where the hell were all the other people I invited to be my *friend*? Granted, it had been only about three hours since I finished sending off the requests, but this was Friendster! Why the hell weren't people checking their Friendster account every other minute? And, if they were, while the hell hadn't they accepted me yet? Like I said, I was the

THE DEATH OF HUMAN INTERACTION

cool, witty guy with a phat (that's right, P-H-A-T) profile using a picture of Jason Biggs, the world's biggest movie star (the PIE FUCKER for Christ's sake), whom I happened to looked exactly like!

From my experience, I identified five common social networking dilemmas:

1. *Social networking causes anxiety.* People want to know what other people are doing at that very moment; they want to be connected and have up-to-date information about you accessible at their fingertips. In my personal Friendster story, I wanted to know where my (supposed) *friends* to whom I sent invitations were at that very moment. If they weren't checking their account to see my invitations, what were they doing?

2. *Social networking can strain friendships.* One of the people I sent an invitation to might have seen my friend request but decided to ignore it. Perhaps they wanted only a select few people to be their *friends*. While that notion is reasonable, why the hell was I not one of those select few? After all, I invited you to be one of my select few (100) *friends*.

3. *Social networking can lead to awkward interactions in the real world.* While it is easy to discriminate amongst people you know (potential *friends*) online, you might still see that person on a random occasion, even if it's a person you never thought you'd see again. About a day or so after I sent out that batch of 75-100 *friend* requests, I ran into a person I had not yet invited. (Let's call him "Albert.") Albert and I bumped into each other at the mall, and we quickly engaged in small talk. We were both all smiles at first until Albert turned the conversation to Friendster. At this point, my face grew pale; after all, while searching for *friends*, I had noticed Albert was friends with Veronica. I could have easily invited Albert to be my friend when I invited Veronica, but I didn't. It was not a malicious

act; it was just a moment of exclusion. I didn't want to invite just anybody to be my *friend*. I hardly even knew Albert that well. Albert went on and asked me if I had joined Friendster. I indicated that I had heard about it once or twice (but deep down I was a Friendster addict!). He then noted that he and our common friend, Veronica, had both recently created profiles and that he had seen that I was one of Veronica's *friends*. I had been caught in a lie. I then broke into a quick sprint away from Albert.

4. *Social networking leads to unnecessary apologies.* Days later when I saw Albert again, I apologized to him for my lie. Then I apologized to him again for not yet befriending him and promised that the next moment I was even within the vicinity of the Internet, I would invite him to be my *friend*. (This was conveniently before everyone had the Internet on their cell phones, so I wouldn't be expected to do it at that exact moment.) By the time I bumped into him again TWO WEEKS LATER at Veronica's birthday party, I had not yet invited Albert to be my friend.

5. *Social networking causes people to lie.* When I saw Albert at Veronica's party, I told him I had not been within the vicinity of the Internet in the past two weeks since I last saw him. I told him I would head home directly after the party, log on to Friendster, and send him a *friend* invitation. This was clearly another lie. Albert and I never became *friends*. I never really liked Albert in the first place!

Despite all the good that Abram and MacKinnon's creation, Friendster, did for the world in bringing people together in a very natural setting (through the Internet), approximately two years after I first signed on, I deleted my profile. Friendster had served its purpose in my life. It was time to move on to bigger and better things. It was time to invite hackers, spam, and terrible profile songs into my social networking world. It was time for MySpace!

EIGHTEEN

Let The World Rejoice; Myspace Is Dead

Friendster may have had its downsides and, as the first of its kind, should bear loads of scrutiny, but it won't go down as one of the worst social media programs ever. MySpace, on the other hand, just plain old sucked!

MySpace is dead. Victory to the spammers, hackers, and, generally, all people of the world!

Well, MySpace isn't technically dead YET, but it is on severe life support. The website that used to be one of the top 10 in the world in terms of daily traffic and, once upon a time, the most popular social networking site, has fallen far. I wouldn't equate it to the fall of the Roman Empire because its dynasty lasted such a short time, but within the social networking realm, it is a good analogy.

Once upon a time, you weren't cool unless you were on MySpace. That was the place where you went to be connected to your friends near and far. It was the place where you could put your personality on display (because, honestly, your friends and acquaintances would NEVER EVER EVER be able to get a good enough sense of who you are by simply hanging out with you).

MySpace allowed you, for the first time in human history, to show others in a very *natural* arena how colorful (or bland) you are as a person. You could design your profile page however you'd like. You could choose default settings that MySpace provided you, or you could build your own. Your profile background could be filled with lightning bolts to show off your electric side, pictures of puppies to show the ladies that you are a sensitive man, or an image of the U.S. Constitution to indicate that you are astute, knowledgeable, and serious. (Again, these are all things that someone CLEARLY would not be able to discover about you via in-person interactions.)

In addition to the fun backgrounds you could design, MySpace gave you the opportunity to correlate a song to your profile page (something that Facebook still does not do to this day—probably for good reason). It was always GREAT opening up someone's MySpace profile page while at work (a place where you shouldn't be dicking around on it), forgetting to turn the volume on your computer down, then hearing Motley Crüe, Toni Braxton, or Hanson blast through your speakers for all your cubicle neighbors to hear. Embarrassing, right? (Not if it was Hanson!)

As you can probably guess, having made it through so many chapters in this book, I definitely was never one of the cool kids that styled up my MySpace profile page. I was (and still am) a social butterfly; hence, I definitely whored myself out to pad my friend count on the site. However, I never felt the need to strip myself of all forms of dignity and create a profile page a teenage girl would be proud of. To be brief (something you'll hardly find in this book), I never grew to love MySpace. In its heydey, it was a time-suck and an underwhelming product that allowed far too much spam to pass through. It also had no class to it; it was a cheap thrill ride for a lot of dumbasses—including yours truly. (The site only degraded in this regard when Rupert Murdoch's NewsCorp added it to his evil empire.)

THE DEATH OF HUMAN INTERACTION

A few years ago, like millions of other folks that finally came to their senses, I rid myself of MySpace altogether. The day I deleted my account was one filled with great relief for a couple reasons: (1) I was no longer associated with such a shitty website (at least this shitty website, not shitty websites altogether ... I love you ChuckNorrisFacts.com), and (2) I regained the hours of 10 p.m. to 1 a.m. in my life—until I joined Facebook. (Please read chapter 19 to learn more.) MySpace, whether or not you are truly dead, you are dead to me—and I feel no remorse!

Despite the first line of this chapter, MySpace is not dead; it is far from it. Apparently Justin Timberlake recently became a part owner of the website. If he can bring "sexy" back, he certainly can do the same for MySpace!

NINETEEN

Where Can I Score Me Some Facebook?

Friendster and MySpace both saw their high points come and quickly fade. Facebook, however, is like herpes ... you can continue to try but you'll never get rid of it!

For any highly sensitive Facebook users, you should consider skipping chapters 19 through 21. These chapters may include some hurtful thoughts. In fact, as we continue in our pursuit of reestablishing natural human interaction in the world (and for the sake of our friendship), I strongly recommend such individuals skip ahead to chapter 22, "Cheaters Never Prosper ... Except Online."

I started writing this chapter a year ago, got distracted for an instant, and wound up on Facebook. Needless to say, one year later, 1,000 friends stronger, and 15,000 wall posts richer, I am back from the abyss.

Facebook is one of the most interesting distractions of the modern day. It is something that has certainly driven a rift between human kind and the pursuit of natural communication. I'd even go so far as to suggest that it is a drug. Let me emphasize that. Facebook is a DRUG. It is a drug that is so potentially harmful that it should be regulated by the FDA. Should we consider selling it via prescriptions at pharmacies? Perhaps, but the reality is Facebook is to our generation what marijuana was to that of our parents'. It's a drug that everyone is using, but most don't want to admit to it.

Let's pretend that one day you're talking to your friend; let's call him Bob. You ask Bob straight-up if he has been using Facebook; Bob gently replies "no." Then you confront Bob with his list of hundreds of friends and his detailed profile including photos, groups to which he belongs, and pages of which he is a fan. He tells you that his girlfriend set up his account and has been using it behind his back; he doesn't know when she started it, but he's a supportive boyfriend and compliant to her habits ... good or bad.

Bob suggests that he is an honest person with a future in politics or business; you can't disagree there. Bob insists that he can't start using Facebook, not now—it would ruin his career. Again, Bob makes a valid point. After all, remember what it did to your coworker's (Tom's) career? One photo from a drunken night back in college found its way to Facebook last year and completely ruined his standing and reputation within the company. Tom was in line to be the youngest director in the company's history; instead, he is today known as the "furry bloused night walker."

As you come back from this side thought, you realize that Bob doesn't even have a girlfriend. Could it be that Bob has lied to you? He has, and as long as he is using Facebook, he will do it again and again. People believe that because it lacks nicotine, Facebook is not addictive and certainly not a drug. Such enablers are blind to the realities and they need to open their eyes. People you care about are in harm's way. To the users, I think it is time to come clean with this addiction. It is time to begin seeking support groups (and don't even think of using Facebook support groups to combat this addiction)!

When I was 19 years old, my parents told me that in the later 1960s and early 1970s they often got stoned. Through college and med school, my father smoked "doobies." (I have heard nothing funnier in my life than hearing that word come out of my father's mouth.) During the same time period, my mom was rolling joints. As my parents had always been big antidrug and antialcohol advocates through my

THE DEATH OF HUMAN INTERACTION

formative years, this came as a huge shock. They had always deterred me from hanging out with my "pot head" friends, so it's easy to understand why I considered them hypocrites ... well, at least until I got stoned that night. I quickly got over it.

This experience did get me thinking about how I would one day be a parent. On one hand, I could act differently than my parents, encouraging my children to act sensibly and reasonably if they did do drugs. Then I realized that my parents' approach seemed way more fun.

I imagine that when I have children, Facebook will be the drug I will criticize them for using. I will forbid them to use Facebook as if it is the worst thing they could possibly do. Every time they turn on the computer and open Internet Explorer, they will think twice about typing "w-w-w-.-f-a-c-..." Every creak of the hardwood floor outside their room will make them jump and quickly navigate their way to CNN.com, ESPN.com, or Wikipedia.com. They will do this because it will be engrained in them that the use of Facebook is a severe letdown to their father. They will feel guilty for even considering using it. (Jewish guilt is a bitch.)

All their friends will notice the extreme paranoia they have toward Facebook. They will be asked in school if they read so-and-so's wall post that this boy is now dating that girl. They will miss invites to their friends' parties that were sent out over Facebook (which could solve some other problems for a father). I will tell them that it is okay to use alternatives to Facebook, like LinkedIn; after all, it is about time they started focusing on their career. My children will grow up with a serious social handicap caused entirely by their self-righteous father.

Then, one day when they are old enough, I will sit them down and blow their minds. I will tell them about how I (yes, I, their father) used Facebook all throughout my mid-20s, and that I am still a closet Facebook user. To cover my trail through the years, I will use Facebook only at the office. My wife will be a big user too. In fact, I will tell them that I met their mother on Facebook (though it's not true). This story of how we met will be a secret to my children through all those years. But, as I move on through life, I will begin to see the light at the end of the tunnel. It will be time for me to reveal the truth and await either a good laugh or serious cry. Either way, keep an eye on my wall posts. That way you will know when the day has come and you can share in the fun.

While I realize that this may seem cruel—creating a near-certain situation where my children will end up in therapy—it's not entirely bad. My kids will get out the door more often. (Granted, it may be to do more traditional recreational drugs.) The fresh air will be good for them (even if they are surrounded by a cloud of smoke).

Some may argue that I will have done it solely for my own kicks. That is true, but then again, I will be Dad. Everyone knows that Dad is always right.

For those of you confused by the implications of this chapter, I should clarify that Facebook is not a real drug. I have simply described it metaphorically. For any stoners that read this book, having possibly burned one too many brain cells, I should note that Facebook is not something that you can put into a bong and smoke ... though I sure would like to see you try. If you can ever figure out how to do that, be sure to take a picture and post it to Facebook. You know I'll be checking daily.

TWENTY

Facebook: Relationship Status

In addition to its addictive nature, Facebook has created undue social pressures that no one should have to experience.

A long, long time ago, man ruled the world. At least, that is the claim that father has told son from generation to generation. The reality is, though, man has never truly ruled the world ... woman has. Women have been setting rules (known and unknown) and testing men since the dawn of time. Women are shrewd, attentive creatures. Men are simple primates who wander the Earth in search of indulgences. This reality WAS bound to be true for eternity. Then, one day, a noble man named Al Gore came along.

Gore, a hero in his own right, created something so wonderful, so magical, and so fantastic that it broke men free from the shackles in which women had them imprisoned. Mr. Gore invented the Internet (better known as the World Wide Web). Let it be known that I believe Mr. Gore should forever be remembered in the history books as the first true leader of men—a George Washington of sorts—in the age-old battle of the sexes. For men, in this battle in which they had never once tasted victory, the World Wide Web offered hope.

What Gore created was a virtual world within our world. A man in a happy and loving relationship who just needed an escape every so often from the boss (his wife, fiancée, girlfriend, mistress, etc.) could plug in, sign on, and explore. Man could take a stroll through cyberspace while the boss was in the other room watching Oprah. He could flirt with multiple women at once and have lengthy, detailed correspondence (in layman's terms, *dirty talk*) for hours with random women he met in chat rooms with names like "Jazz Lovers," "Poetry Enthusiasts," and "50 and Older Sex-A-Holics." It didn't matter to him that *SexyBecky123* was actually 45-year-old Floyd Johnson, firefighter and father of four from Aberdeen, South Dakota. Little did he care that *LustyLady456* was 500-pound Laura Lanahan from Albuquerque, New Mexico. Little did he imagine that *HotRhonda78* would be 78-year-old Rhonda Bickerstein of Newark, New Jersey, America Online's newest member and Shady Acres Retirement Community's most tech-savvy resident. Man ruled this virtual world. And, when he was done for the night, ready to return to the real world, he could crawl into bed and snuggle up next to the boss.

Then one day, only a few years ago, Mr. Gore's evident arch nemesis, a young, naïve boy named Mark Zuckerberg, came along. Mark, raised by a pack of wild, hairy feminists in a laboratory deep within the Sierra Nevadas in California, was taught since birth that man, given his eerie similarities to a chimpanzee, should never be allowed to have the upper hand. Mark plotted for years to destroy that power created by Gore. As a teenager, he would stay up till all hours of the night, an obsessed insomniac.

Then one day, as he approached the edge of insanity, it hit him. The idea was Facebook. Mark would use Gore's own invention against him and created what we call today "social networking," a comprehensive website that allows friends to communicate with friends through the World Wide Web—but not only that. These friends would have the capability to share comments, photos, profiles, etc. Everyone who created an account on Facebook (which everyone in the world would do … refer to chapter 19) would have the capability to view other

THE DEATH OF HUMAN INTERACTION

people's information. This meant no more secrets. This meant transparency. This meant a return to days of old and the seemingly imminent loss in the battle of the sexes for man. However, Zuckerberg's Facebook needed more.

So Zuckerberg included a feature that allowed others to post pictures on your Facebook page, pictures that told a story, but the story they told could always be played off as something else. "No, Honey ... that's just my friend (or cousin or ex-girlfriend) whose picture I've been meaning to un-tag for months." However, the real evil that Zucker-Dick forced upon men was the "Relationship Status." This feature complicated the world of man to an unimaginable level. Now and forever, man would have to explain himself to woman, fielding questions such as:

Assuming a "Single" status:
- "Aren't we in a relationship?"
- "How long have we been together? So why aren't we in a relationship yet?"
- "You don't want to see anyone else, right?"
- "Don't you love me?"
- ➢ Problem 1 with these questions is that no guy in his right mind remembers specific dates and women aren't interested in hearing an approximation.
- ➢ Problem 2 is these questions force a guy into a relationship he probably didn't want in the first place, ultimately leading to either a long, unhappy marriage or an ugly breakup.

Assuming an "In a Relationship" status:
- "You mean you have a girlfriend?"
- "Why didn't you link your *In a Relationship* status to display my name? Are you embarrassed by me?"
- "Does your girlfriend swing?"
- "Dude, did you know I used to get booty calls from your girlfriend?"

- "Wait, the two of you just broke up?"
- "Wait, did you just break up with me using the Facebook 'Relationship Status'?"
- ➢ Problem 1 with these questions is it is always uncomfortable to find out your girlfriend used to sleep with one of your friends. I'd rather not know ... thanks again, Zucker-Dick!
- ➢ Problem 2 is you have to field responses to the same question a hundred times after a breakup thanks to Facebook's "News Feed."
- ➢ Problem 3 is that it is the awkward conversation you have to have with someone after informing them that you did, in fact, just break up with them over Facebook by way of "Relationship Status."

Truth be told, I personally have not had to field these types of questions very often though my friends haven't always been so lucky. I learned the perils of the "Relationship Status" feature early on. In fact, I haven't posted a status since I broke up with an ex-girlfriend nearly five years ago. The questions are obnoxious, annoying, and unnecessary. Who wants to be bombarded with such inquiries while on the brink of depression following a bad breakup? It wasn't long after that breakup that I swore to myself I would not even consider changing my status again until after 10 years of marriage and/or my wife was pregnant with our third child. At that point, I figure it is safe to say that I am in a relationship.

It's kind of sad how powerful the "Relationship Status" feature has become. With over 1 billion Facebook users worldwide, most people are likely to have more than 100 Facebook friends. That means when you change your status to *In a Relationship,* 100+ people are suddenly informed that you are now in a relationship with *Jennifer Barnes*. And, when you and Jennifer break up, 100+ people immediately know the personally emotional news that you and Jennifer are no longer in a relationship. Most people never asked to or never wanted to live in a public spotlight; however, Facebook encourages everyone that signs on to live in a public spotlight through features like "Relationship Status," causing unnecessary pressures for people that never wanted that burden.

I'm not suggesting that all of Facebook is bad. After all, it is nice to be able to share stories and pictures with family and friends while traveling or to reconnect with old friends from the past that you no longer live near. However, I strongly believe the "Relationship Status" feature is something the world could do without.

As if the world of dating isn't pressurized enough, Facebook intensified it. But that's not the only personal drama they have created.

TWENTY ONE

Facebook: A Family Divide

There may be a million fish in the sea, but you have only one (blood) family, and your Facebook habits may or may not have pissed them off. This is what I like to call unnecessary drama—the thing my mother lives for!!

A few weeks ago, I was told a story that filled me with pity, yes pity, for the girl who told it (let's call her Kristy) and her (shitty) communication competence.

Kristy, a 23-year-old girl, has a 20-year-old brother. Throughout their childhoods, the two never got along. I found this to be fairly easy to relate to as my brother Marc and I always knew how to piss each other off. She told me she wished she could have a close relationship with him now that they are grown (despite living at separate ends of the country)—a reasonable notion and one I can sympathize with as I believe that positive family relationships are valuable. However, no matter how hard she tried through the past year, her brother would not talk with her, not even for a few minutes over the phone. This deeply saddened her, and it touched me. (Again, I believe family bonds are incredibly important.)

I decided I wasn't going to let the conversation die there (teary-eyed and reaching for a Kleenex); I needed to dig deeper. While I don't consider myself an expert, I do know how to communicate with my siblings. I figured perhaps I could get to the root of the problem and then offer sound advice.

I asked Kristy, "In what capacity do you try to contact your brother? Do you try to call him often?"

"No. Not really. I generally ask my mom to put him on the phone when I'm done talking with her."

Okay. She offers him slopping phone seconds—not the best approach, though also not detrimental. "Well, have you ever expressed to him your feelings in writing, perhaps drafted a letter on a sheet of paper, stuck it in an envelope, and sent it to him via snail mail? Or have you ever sent him a card?"

With pain in her voice, she replied, "I tried to befriend him on Facebook once. Oh, and I posted a message on his wall. He totally ignored me. My brother denied my friendship!"

At that point in our conversation, as you can hopefully imagine, I jumped back within my brain so far that I nearly smashed through the wall 10 feet behind me. The sadness and compassion I had been feeling for her turned to sheer pity. I tried to pull a few rational thoughts together, some words that could send her off in the right direction. However, she and I were people of two different worlds. I came from the planet where you tell people how you feel. She came from the planet where you blatantly hide any sense of true emotion behind walls of technology; she came from the "Not Found Generation" (refer to chapter 1).

It is still tough for me to fathom that Kristy truly believed that all the animosity she and her brother felt toward each other through their entire lives would be remedied by befriending her brother ON FACEBOOK and sending him a public message such as "hi" or "I miss

THE DEATH OF HUMAN INTERACTION

you!" or "Que pasa?" Has today's world actually reached the point where we must rely on non-intimate forms of technology in order to communicate? What does this portend for our future? Are people with the ability to express their feelings a dying breed?

"Kristy," I told her, "listen hard. Everything, and I mean EVERYTHING, you are doing to connect with your brother is absurd [perhaps a little harsh, I know, though necessary in this situation]. Do you ask yourself in the morning if you really want a close relationship with him? If so, do you honestly believe that Facebook is the best forum of communication? Can you look me in the eyes and tell me you believe the approach you are taking is actually going to resolve your issues?"

"Ummmm." Her face looked frozen.

"Here's what you do ... STOP USING FACEBOOK TO REBUILD YOUR RELATIONSHIP! Call your brother. If he won't answer, write him a card and send it in the mail. If you don't remember how to use a postage stamp, send him an e-mail, but do not ... I repeat ... do not send it through Facebook! Show your brother that he means more to you than a momentary thought."

After all, isn't that what communication on Facebook is—a momentary thought? When you sign on to Facebook, you are overloaded with information regarding every person that you may or may not know on your friend list, so much so that you are hit with immediate ADD. If that's the case, what does it say to a loved one, whom you are trying to reconnect with after years of bickering, when your apology is a passing thought? If I were her brother, I wouldn't be responsive either.

Kristy didn't know how to respond. She looked slightly puzzled. Maybe I shouldn't have offered all this advice in Spanish. In retrospect, I believe her native tongue is English.

Yes ... Facebook Really Does Destroy Families

For as much as Facebook can keep families apart, it can also tear them apart. (Remember, Mom, I love you very much!) There are just certain places in life where a son should be allowed keep his distance from his Jewish mother. For example, I would never take my mother to work with me as she would explain to my boss that I deserve a promotion because I'm such a good boy. I would never take my mom drinking with my guy friends as I would end up getting my mouth washed out with soap by the end of the night. I put Facebook into this same category.

I have plenty of friends who have crossed that boundary with both their parents with little regret. First, I generally express to those friends a very sarcastic "congratulations" (suckers!). Second, I remind them that their mother probably isn't Jewish. (For those of you who don't know from experience, Jewish mothers are protective, intrusive, and slightly crazy. ... Mom, again, remember I love you.) Third, I tell them that I am the youngest of three boys, and clearly my mother's "little boy." A Jewish mother's children are the most important people in the world to her; that means, in my case, my Dad is the fourth most important person in the world to my Mom (fifth, if you count the dog as a person, which my Mom usually does).

What that means is that no matter how far away from them you are in the world, they will know what you are doing at that very second ... and most of that is based on instinct. (For example, my mother knows that I am presently writing something for public viewing that she will hold against me for the rest of my life.) When you offer technology like Facebook to a Jewish mother, the possibility of her exerting control over your life is limitless. If I want to continue to maintain a slice of independence from my mother, if I want to keep that umbilical cord detached, I cannot—I will not—accept her as a friend on Facebook. (Please do not judge me harshly until you have completed this chapter. Then, you can call me an "ass.")

The moment that I befriend my mother, she will look through my profile, read every single wall post, look at every single picture, and

THE DEATH OF HUMAN INTERACTION

browse through my list of friends. She will notice my ex-girlfriend as a friend and ask me for the one millionth time if I am going to get back together with her; no, Mom ... I'm married. (To be fair to my Mom, I originally wrote this before I was in a relationship with my wife.) She'll see a "Happy Birthday" post from an old friend of mine from high school that she never liked and criticize me for ever having been friends with such a pothead. She will ask me why there aren't more pictures of her and me in my photo albums, requiring me to remind her that she doesn't like to be photographed. And, if she ever sees me write a tasteless "Status Update," she won't hesitate to pick up the phone and yell at me. She'll have done this all out of love; that doesn't mean she won't give me high blood pressure by my early thirties.

You may ask, "You can't just not friend her, can you?" That's a very valid question. The answer is "not entirely" and "yes." In the past year, my mother has tried to friend me seven times; the year before that, eighteen times; the year before that, thirty-seven times. I have ignored her each and every time ... not without a heap of guilt. At the end of the day, for the sake of my sanity, I realize it is for the best. When she gets upset at me (she gets very upset at times), I tell her that she is better than any friend that I have on Facebook. I reassure her of the bond between mother and son, confirming that ours is stronger than any other. I tell her that she is my super-secret friend; she is the only one in the world with that status. She is such a secret friend that she doesn't even have access to any bit of my profile (unlike my other friends). I'll give my mom credit; she sees right through my sneaky ploy. She knows that I'm a bullshitter; after all, I got that talent from her.

At the end of the day, I acknowledge that my mother is smarter than me. That leads me to believe that (a) no matter how hard I try to keep her from gaining my friend status on Facebook, she will guilt her way there (never underestimate the power of Jewish guilt from mother to son), (b) she may already have access to my Facebook through other means, or (c) she keeps me distracted by asking about Facebook and already knows all. For now, I will continue to keep her as my super-secret friend.

Mom, I am sorry for everything I wrote in this chapter! I love you and look forward to getting my annual pair of slippers that you buy me every Hanukkah!

TWENTY TWO

Cheaters Never Prosper ... Except Online

Facebook (and social media in general) may make relationships awkward and break up families, but it does in fact have at least one redeeming quality ...

Through the years, one key lesson instilled upon my generation is to always *Play Fair*. "Winners never cheat," "Cheaters never prosper," and "Never play poker against a man named after a city." (Wait ... the last one isn't meant for this chapter at all.) We were raised (at least our parents would like to believe) with a healthy dose of morals and character. If we weren't, it would reflect poorly on them as caretakers and shapers of our lives. In my case, my parents used Jewish guilt to drive home this point.

In general, my parents did a great job. I never once cheated on my taxes, used performance-enhancing drugs during my little league baseball career, nor rigged a beauty pageant (although this last one is on my bucket list). However, during my formative years, cheating was less of an option. It wasn't that my friends and I didn't have the will to cheat; we simply didn't have the means (especially for a bunch of lazy asses like us. Don't forget, the Internet didn't start entering homes until I was already a teenager.)

Not anymore! Today, with easy access to a plethora of information, cheaters, liars, fakes, and phonies aren't just welcomed, they're handed the keys to the vault. I know this because I have turned from a morally sound, good Jewish boy into a ruthless, scamming adult with one thought in mind ... WINNING BIG!

You may be getting the idea that I have gotten into some very bad stuff and am perhaps in way over my head. Not the case. I still do not intend to serve any jail time, at least not until I slide farther down the slippery slope. Plus, I need to bulk up a bit before getting to that point; I imagine it's way more fun to be "the butch" than "the bitch."

Do you remember the good ole days when family and friends would sit down in the den, open up a classic board game like Clue, Monopoly, Trivial Pursuit, or Pictionary, and in a competitive but friendly spirit play for hours with loads of laughs along the way? There would be some jeering and teasing throughout, but smiles and appreciation for one another at the end of the game. (Of course, there were people like my brother Marc who would steal money from the bank in Monopoly, but since he was sitting right in front of us while he did it, we would decide to all team up on him.) For the most part, the game was played in a fair and honest setting.

Those days are long gone. Like everything else, all the classic games have moved online. You no longer have to sit in the same room with another person to compete with them in a game. That also means all participants must be more trusting of their opponent(s).

It's funny how quickly integrity disappears when playing a game on the Internet, a game with no consequences. For example, during my first year of graduate school in the fall of 2007, I started using Facebook. My friends and I, slightly later bloomers to that fad, all created accounts around the same time. Almost immediately after joining, we all also grew addicted to a Scrabble Facebook app; our favorite time to play, obviously, was during class. (If you don't believe me, ask

THE DEATH OF HUMAN INTERACTION

my managerial accounting professor. I mean, why would we pay attention to the person in the front of the room that we were compensating so greatly?) We all loved this app so much because our scores would immediately post publicly online, which led to embarrassing amounts of bragging.

A confession pertinent to the story and to the point of this chapter is that I suck at Scrabble. In fact, I could possibly be one of the worst Scrabble players alive today. As you can tell by reading this book, I am not a wordsmith. In fact, I think I scored about 200 points less on my SAT verbal score than on my math (which leads me to question how I ended up with a communications degree and writing a book as opposed to an engineering degree and writing code in a dark room somewhere). In Scrabble, I tend to stick to three- or four-letter words. Despite my unimpressive abilities, I still have a fiery, competitive ego to satisfy. And, even more so, I enjoy watching a friend's even greater pride shatter.

On one occasion, I locked into a game with a classmate named Greg Smiley. (I changed his name in hopes that he doesn't try to sue for slander.) Greg had one of the biggest heads of any of my classmates (both literally and figuratively), which is quite impressive amongst 115 type-A, MBA students. (He also happened to be our class president—and telling you this may have just destroyed my slander defense.) In this particular game, Greg was kicking my butt and bragging nonstop. He was also incredibly proud of the 19-1 record he built (that one loss coming against his wife who threatened to hold out sex if he didn't let her win). Something had to be done, but I knew I couldn't rely on my simple brain in this instance. I needed to cheat; I needed the Internet.

Through a quick Internet search, I found a website built specifically for Scrabble cheaters like me. All I had to do was enter all my letters and click "enter." Instantly, the website generated all the words that could be made using those letters as well as the associated scores! During my first use of this website, the program proved its value by providing me with such a ridiculous eight-letter word that I could not define it at the time and, to this day, cannot even remember what it was. That word put me so far ahead; all Greg Smiley could do was eat my dust. Obviously, despite all my denials (even if he reads this book, I'll still deny it), he knew I cheated. It didn't matter; his record fell to 19-2. It was a dismal moment for him; everyone could see that I beat him. That frustrated the hell out of him and, well, his frustration put a huge smile on my face.

The lessons of our parents are good ones. We shouldn't cheat ... well, not for the most part. When competing in a harmless online game against a guy like Greg Smiley in a battle of egos, I say, "What the hell? Why not?"

Thank you, Internet!

TWENTY THREE

Linkedin: Not So Bad

Over the past several chapters, you may have picked up my slightly (very) negative attitude toward social media. That attitude comes with good reason: I just don't really see the overarching value in it. There are some things that I can point to here and there in Facebook or its predecessors that are nice (for example, event invitations); however, most other things are shitty wastes of time. LinkedIn, on the other hand ...

Surprisingly, despite my feelings toward Friendster, MySpace, and Facebook, I have minimal negative comments to make regarding LinkedIn. Of all the social networking sites, I believe it negatively impacts our lives the least (which is about as "glass half-full" as I can get when it comes to social media). People who use LinkedIn do so for legitimate purposes: to make business connections, advance their careers, or try to find jobs. They get on, take care of business, and get off quite painlessly. Sometimes they mosey around, but that's because they're deep in the job search and need to find a source of income because their parents or landlord or both are close to kicking them to the curb. (I can't fault them for that. Can you?)

It's not like people log on to LinkedIn to get daily status updates on their connections, look through an endless number of photos that all look the same (some dumbass wasted with their friends, some beautiful sunset, some stupid picture of their stupid baby—I might have crossed a line; I take that last one back), and play around with the great abyss. People's use of LinkedIn is actually both functional and reasonable.

Now you may say, "WHHOOOOOOOOOOOOAAAAAA! WAIT A DAMN MINUTE. You're letting these guys off pretty easily. I mean, you equated Mark Zuckerberg with an evil feminine mastermind and basically called the Friendster guys friendless dipshits. You're just going to let Reid Hoffman and company slide?" The answer is "yes" and here are my reasons why:

- I use LinkedIn for all the reasons I mentioned above and it has helped me advance my career more times than not. It has a legitimate purpose and makes sense to me!

- I did several Google searches on Reid Hoffman to find out more about the skeletons in his closet and everything came back clean. Some of these searches included:
    - Reid Hoffman Yankees fan (Reid isn't a completely twisted bastard. I don't think he's into sports, but if he was, he wouldn't be a Yankees fan, thankfully!)
    - Reid Hoffman cat owner (Again, Reid IS NOT a completely twisted bastard. He's a dog person.)
    - Reid Hoffman anarchist (He was offered a board membership for WikiLeaks but decided he preferred to keep his soul.)
    - Reid Hoffman Saddam Hussein (Reid studied abroad in Iraq in '87, but never met the guy.)
    - Reid Hoffman Canadian (Google turned back some odd results for Reid's love of Canadian bacon.)
    - Reid Hoffman Georgetown (You'd understand this one if you were a Syracuse alum like me; shame on you for not going to the greatest university in the world!)
    - Reid Hoffman Nazi (It turns out that Reid is Jewish.)

THE DEATH OF HUMAN INTERACTION

- ○ Reid Hoffman Justin Bieber (Reid walked away from a White Elephant exchange with the album *Under the Mistletoe* but never personally bought one of Justin's albums. There are witnesses to vouch for him. On a side note, Reid was flustered by the album as he had never celebrated Christmas and was unfamiliar with mistletoe.)
  - ○ Reid Hoffman serial killer (He went to Stanford, not Harvard like Ted Kaczynski.)

- He seems like he is dealing with some other struggles in his life, namely his overindulgence of sweets.

- LinkedIn does not consume our lives! There is a simple question you must ask yourself: "Do you use LinkedIn by choice to fulfill a purpose or do you use it because it scratches an itch?" I wholeheartedly believe that 99.99999999999 percent of people would say the former. However, can they say the same about Facebook? About Twitter? HELL NO! Simply put … Facebook and Twitter are obsessions; LinkedIn is not.

In conclusion:

➢ Facebook, MySpace, Friendster, Twitter, and all the others = bad
➢ LinkedIn = not so bad

Reid, you have received formal Panzer approval (at least to an extent).

TWENTY FOUR

Twitter ... Really?

I was harsh on all forms of social media (and Reid Hoffman's diet) up to this point with the exception of LinkedIn. Does Twitter suck too?

Twitter ... I've never used it and don't plan to. As if the news world hasn't gotten bad enough, now Twitter exists at the core of our existence as the ULTIMATE news feed. Does no one else see anything wrong with this? Twitter allows the use of 140 characters to broadcast a news story to the world; and—the worst part—anyone and everyone is a journalist! (I've tried to avoid cursing as much as possible throughout this book; however, please allow me to ask/exclaim ... WHAT THE FUCK?) As if 24/7 news (I'll dive into this more in chapter 31) and Facebook posts weren't bad enough, now the world has something that has solidified itself in our society and in our lives that provides an endless flow of irrelevant and nonsensical news stories. Since I have never used Twitter (I only learned about how it works through others), here are some examples of news "tweets" that I imagine get "tweeted" quite frequently:

1. New boobs, new jeans, new attitude!! ☺
2. C+ on Mr Hamper-assfaces algebra exam. Six tries the charm to pass 8th grade! High school...its on! Booooom!!!

3. Mr Bootsy, the world's cutest most adorable cat, is playing with his toy mouse… Awww!!
4. Saw God this morning on the corner of 5th and Main. Didn't realize that she is black.
5. Who the hell names their cat "Mr Bootsy?"
6. Just read Vanity Fair on the bus.
7. Just watched someone on the bus read Vanity Fair.
8. Just noticed someone watching another person read Vanity Fair while on the bus.
9. I was the one who watched you read Vanity Fair while on the bus.
10. You're following me on Twitter while stalking me on the bus while I read Vanity Fair.
11. Yes. Vanity Fair looks like a great read!
12. Vanity Fair is a great read!
13. Been thinking all day that I haven't had a chance to tweet since this morning…
14. I just trimmed my ball hairs…
15. "I'm coo coo for Cocoa Puffs!" I haven't heard that saying in forever!
16. Lindsay Lohan – back to jail AGAIN…

As you read through all those tweets, what did you think to yourself? Did you think, "Haaa … that's funny?" or did you think, "Why the hell am I interested in knowing any of this?" If you thought the former, first off, thank you for the laughter (Dad); I'm working hard on my various jokes throughout the book and now know that they are paying off on you (Dad). Secondly, you're a lost soul with no chance to rebound and diminish the control that technology has over you and your life so you might as well give up. At the same time, you've already paid for the book (unless you borrowed it from your local library, in which case, good for you … bad for me—and my royalty checks); you might as well finish reading (although I want to reiterate that you have no chance of changing your habits … NONE WHATSOEVER!). If you thought the latter ("Why the hell am I interested in knowing any of this?"), you are

THE DEATH OF HUMAN INTERACTION

my type of person; I can promise that you have a chance in my ideal world (please refer back to the Preface "My Ideal World")!

Honestly, for all the millions of people out there that use Twitter frequently, don't you have something better to do with your time? (Sorry, babe. I know you use it for work.) I constantly find myself surrounded by people on the bus during morning and evening commutes to and from work that are tweeting endlessly. As I pointed out above, tweeters have nothing of relevance to say, but they want to say it anyway because they want to be heard. Now, let me clarify, they don't want to be heard by the people who are physically close to them, whether it is someone they know or a complete stranger; they desire to be heard through their technology, to tell everyone "following" them on Twitter what they feel or what they are doing at that exact moment. They prefer to be heard via technology as opposed to in person because they can always hide behind it; if someone confronts or challenges what they say, they can simply ignore it. It's almost a way to spark conversation or debate without being held accountable for following through. If you don't like how people respond, you can turn Twitter (or your entire device) off for a while to avoid follow-up.

The funny thing is that society wasn't always like this; society used to be colorful, warm, and welcoming. However, over time, as we have allowed technologies like Twitter into our lives, society has changed (in my opinion, for the worse). People like Jack Dorsey, a Tech Geek by all accounts and one of the creators of Twitter, are introverted and (to their profit) are building new technologies that, though it isn't their purpose, are making most everyone else in society more like them.

I use Jack Dorsey as an example (in part because this chapter is primarily about Twitter) because I recently saw him on a Larry King television special called "Dinner with Kings." At one point during the special, Larry posed a question to his guests about close friends. When he turned to Jack, he admitted to his lack of deeper friendships. While all the other guests—from Conan to Shaq to Tyra Banks—talked about the friendships they've had forever, Jack said "I don't have, um … I don't have close friends that I've been friends with for years and years and years, but recently just gone deeper and deeper with … Um, but, you know, they're grounding, they have perspective, they're inspiring."

My first thought in hearing his response was, "This is not making logical sense from a grammatical standpoint." My second thought was, "I am not surprised." Jack probably spent a good deal of his life sitting in front of his computer disconnected from real society wondering why people didn't understand but taking solace in the fact that he understood all. And, like Mark Zuckerberg, Bill Gates, and Steve Jobs, he wanted the real world to conform to his version of it.

I will also give these men their due; they are all brilliant inventors and innovators. Like Bell, Edison, Franklin, and Tesla before them, they have all changed society, which is not a simple task. The difference between them and their predecessors, however (as I argue), is that the inventions and innovations of their predecessors did more to enhance society than detract from it. For example, the light bulb, which was invented by Edison, has given people around the world the ability to more easily and safely function in darkness. I guarantee that the good that has come with the invention of the light bulb significantly outweighs the bad.

Twitter also has some good and some bad; however, the bad is more substantial. I have already delved into the bad (allow me to reemphasize that IT IS BAD). The good … well, the good comes with relevant news stories or breaking news that can either rally support or guide people toward safety. For example, if someone tweets about a tornado they just saw passing by this road, you will know to stay the hell away from that area. That is good, that is useful, that is worthwhile. However, our human nature is to abuse the bad and neglect the good, which is not something I can blame on Jack Dorsey. What I can blame on him is giving society the tool to exploit our own natural flaws and be warped into a worthless realm of lackluster communication and distraction. I can blame him for contributing to a dumber society that is "less informed of relevant information"!

I apologize if there are some inaccuracies about Twitter in this chapter. Like I said, I have never used Twitter and don't plan to.

Actually I don't really care about the inaccuracies. I take back my apology!

TWENTY FIVE

Grow A Sack And Take A Chance

The desire to use social media is weird to me. Why do they want to interact with people they know in a virtual world when they can do so in the real world? If there is one thing that is even more bizarre, it is online dating. It just seems odd to create a profile, look for matches that meet some certain statistical requirements, and connect in a very manufactured setting. But, to each his own.

I have a few excellent ideas for all of you lonely souls out there:

1. Go to a friend's party. Meet a girl, guy, hermaphrodite—whatever you're into. Instead of spending much (or any) time during the party asking that person (or thing) questions, ask your friend at the end of the night for his/her/its name. Then, go home and look that person up on Facebook. Find out everything you need to know about that person—their likes, their dislikes, their alma mater, where they are from, etc. If you build up enough courage, send them a friend request and awkwardly ask them a few probing questions over Facebook messenger one day. If you don't, continue to Facebook to stalk them for several weeks until the next party where you may be presented with the opportunity to talk to them again. Then if/when you do talk to that person again, ask them if they like poetry (which

you already know because you have been Facebook stalking them), then tell them that you have two tickets to a poetry reading this coming Wednesday. Hint at the notion that it'd be fun to go together. If they are brave enough, they will admit that they'd love to. If not, they will suggest that you friend request them on Facebook and ask them again on there. (And on it goes!)

2. Sign up for Match.com, eHarmony, OkCupid, JDate, or one of the other many dating websites. Peruse the site for several weeks while detailing your perfect mate. For example, mine is a slender, white female college-educated journalist who is five-foot-five and has brown hair and brown eyes, is sassy and loves dogs. (I just described my wife who would kill me if I described anyone different.) When you figure out exactly what you want (in a very mechanical setting), send that person a message introducing yourself. If you are lucky, within a few weeks that person, after doing an extensive online background check on you, will respond to you (hopefully in kind). After several more online interactions (where an individual's personality *clearly* shines through), perhaps one of the two of you will be brave enough to suggest an in-person meeting. (Don't worry; this process takes only several months to get to the first date.)

Both these ideas are very conventional in this day and age. (This is true.) And they are both clearly effective as well. (This is sarcasm—I'm just letting you know in case it doesn't come through clearly enough in my writing.)

It is hilarious to me that in this day and age, the simple notion of striking up a conversation with someone you find attractive and asking for their number and to go out on a date has died. It seems to me that now with the existence of alternatives (i.e., suggestions 1 and 2 above) to this simple process, people no longer have to deal with in-person rejection and humiliation (as if the humiliation is even that bad).

THE DEATH OF HUMAN INTERACTION

I don't care how tough a person is, the desire to feel wanted is part of human nature. As soon as a person feels otherwise, he or she generally puts up barriers as a show of pride. Whether someone is approached online or in person, there is still the possibility you will have to face rejection; however, with online dating/matchmaking, you may not have to deal with the humiliation end of it (at least not to the extent that you would feel when being rejected in person). This begs the questions … Are most people today really that afraid of in-person rejection? Are most people today that fragile? I honestly hope not.

The amazing thing to me is the vast sociological experiment that comes along with online dating. The Internet has truly changed people's habits and approaches. According to some random survey results I found in a NYDailyNews.com article (the second link on a Google results page for a search I just performed) from February 16, 2010, 30 percent of all web users are online dating. (If I gave you any more information about this article, you might begin to question the validity of it, so I will not.)

Just for the sake of figuring out how astronomical that number really is, let's assume that one quarter of the nearly 7 billion people in the world use the Internet; that would mean that 525 million people are online daters. That is absolutely absurd! ABSOLUTELY ABSURD! Twenty years ago, that number was zero, a big fat zero! Beyond 20 years ago, people still met each other somehow, some way; people fell in love, and they got married, had kids, had grandkids, and celebrated golden anniversaries all without the assistance of dating websites. That begs the question … Why has the Internet affected the dating world so dramatically?

The simplest answer to the question above is that online dating is easy. People that use it love the opportunity the Internet provides to do a background check on others. They love to find their right match on paper. They love that they can screen hundreds of people in a matter of minutes instead of *wasting* hours on a date screening only one.

People are busy in today's world (or perceive themselves to be busy). I mean, between work, picking up take-out food, going to the gym, playing video games, shopping online, watching television, and running to Starbucks to get your fifth latte of the day, how are you supposed to find time in your schedule to actually strike up a conversation with a stranger and propose a longer follow-up conversation or perhaps a date? There are clearly just not enough hours in the day.

To all of you that honestly believe these sentiments, I call bullshit on you and your rationale! People have the time; they don't take the initiative and don't have the guts. It's simple. When you meet someone you like, you ask them out. When they say "yes" or some variation of it, you plan out your schedule (prioritize) to make the time to get to know that person. If all goes well with the first date, you can go on a second, third, fourth, fifth, and sixth date. Hell, that person could even be the one.

There are two things that piss me off more than anything else about online dating:

1. There is nothing special about the story of how two people met online. The wonderful stories of how two lovebirds found their way to each other are diminishing, both in terms of romanticism and numbers. I love the story of how I met my wife; I love every time I get to tell it and I can't wait to tell our kids and grandkids someday. (But I feel like we are a dying breed of people fortunate enough to have a good story to tell.) Our story is one of two people who are meant to be together. If we had met each other online, it would in no way be a symbol of one of the strengths of our relationship as our story is ... patience. We have our story because I took a chance one day to talk to her and ask her out on a date, not realizing she had a boyfriend at the time. Two years later, once she became single, we have our story because she in turn took a chance by asking me out on a date (and going after the one she felt she had let slip away, as

she describes it). Our story demonstrates that patience led us to one another and, ultimately, to happiness.

2. Online daters generally lie about how they met their significant other because they are ashamed of it; they're ashamed by the truth even though they have a passion for their significant other. They wish they had a story of interest to tell, so they often make up a story altogether. Very infrequently will they boldly admit that they met their significant other online. I hate liars!

On that note, I should admit that I am a liar too. No, not about the part about how I met my wife and how we ended up together; that part is true. And I haven't lied in this chapter thus far. However, I have lied to numerous friends and family throughout the last few years when asked if I had ever used an online dating site. I must admit once and for all (clearing my conscience) that I have in fact used two online dating sites at two separate times in my life. However, I had good reasons for it.

Winter 2008 – During my first few months in Seattle while I was in graduate school, I started dating a girl that I fell madly in love with. We had a short relationship, one that lasted only four months or so, but it was intense. We got along on every level with one exception—she is Catholic and very religious while I am Jewish and quite agnostic. This difference in our lives was so big that we both realized we either had a rocky future together in the long run or no future whatsoever. We acted on the latter.

Well, after any big breakup, the best thing to do is put yourself back out on the market, right? The problem was, I was new to Seattle, had a small friend base, and felt overwhelmed by the Catholic culture and the intensely religious people my ex had always surrounded me with. I was certainly aching to find people that I could better relate to. (Don't misunderstand me. I have nothing against Catholics. I just had no plans to convert or raise Catholic babies one day.)

Hence, for the first and only time in my life, I yearned to meet Jewish women (which I did regrettably, despite the fact that I knew it would make my mother happy)! For a couple months, I tried JDate. (For those of you unfamiliar with this site, it is a dating site for Jews to meet Jews.) What I discovered is how awkward it is to meet people online. I felt like a sleazy used car salesman trying to sell myself at a higher value. If a girl wanted a guy with a moustache, I would tell her that I had a moustache even though it was clear from my photos that I had no moustache (and I could never physically grow one even if I didn't shave for a year). My biggest problem was that I am a terrible salesperson.

Summer 2009 – I was in my cocky, "I just finished my MBA" and "I'm so pimp" mode. I found myself in a high-paying job living in a nice bachelor pad in a nice neighborhood near downtown Seattle and it was a beautiful summer. I felt good. The problem, however, was that during my time in business school, I had siloed myself so deeply amongst my classmates that I hardly knew any women in Seattle to date and my friends didn't know any women they could introduce me to. Most of my classmates were older and married, so I wasn't going to meet any women through them; I was one of only four people in my class that was single. Plus, having now graduated from school, I was no longer on a college campus on a regular basis—a wonderful place to meet (undergrad) women as my wife will tell you. To top it all off, as I already mentioned, I was living in Seattle. (Seattle, for those of you unfamiliar, is weird in the sense that it probably ranks #1 in the U.S. for cities with the most antisocial, passive-aggressive people per capita. In fact, I guarantee that they blow away the closest competition.) Hence, I decided to give Match.com a try for a couple months. What I discovered is what others had told me for years … Match.com is a great place to go play the field.

Since I tried online dating a second time, you might assume that I enjoyed it the first time around—quite the contrary. In fact, I tried it again more so out of boredom than for any other reason. As I implied

THE DEATH OF HUMAN INTERACTION

in my last comment, what I discovered was that Match.com is truly a place for Players; in fact, I'd probably even call it a player haven.

Think about it: If you have a good enough profile that will attract numerous women to you (or at least pique their interest), then all you have to do is take 15 minutes to respond to 20 e-mails and all the sudden you have dates/hookups for a month. Even the front end of it is easy. Typically, if you go out on a Friday night with intentions to meet someone, you might spend anywhere from two to four hours sparking conversations, going more in depth, and possibly walking away with a telephone number (or you may leave empty-handed). Alternatively, if you spend one to two hours putting together a masterful profile that really sells you in an elegant way, you could find a significantly higher success rate. Essentially, it's a numbers game.

LOCATION-BASED DATING SERVICES

I am not familiar with any of the websites, but I have heard that the newest craze in online dating is location based. Location-based dating services use your smart phone to identify where you are physically located at that given moment. Based on information you previously supplied, it looks for potential matches for you that are within your vicinity—at the same bar, party, park, coffee shop, concert, etc. You can search through your matches to determine if there is anyone you would like to then flirt with ON YOUR PHONE.

So, instead of noticing a girl 10 feet away from you, walking over to her, and sparking a dialogue with her, technology has brought us to the point where you notice a girl 10 feet away from you via a mobile application, do a quick background/profile check on her, then send her a text message.

Does anyone else recognize how sad this is? Honestly, I wish I had some classier advice than … grow a sack and take a chance using no device other than your mouth, your brain, and your body language!

There are two reliable channels to get you laid: (1) yourself, or (2) technology. There is only one way to tempt fate and possibly fall in love: yourself. Again, grow a sack! (For those of you that think I am being a bit harsh and consider me to be a hypocrite, you are correct. I spell this out clearly in chapter 40.)

TWENTY SIX

URBANCOUGAR.COM

From the previous chapter, you may infer that I believe the Internet has a redeeming quality in its ability to help people play the field. Perhaps, but only to a certain extent. However, for those of you who hunt cougars, there are certainly merits to it.

Technology, particularly the Internet, is not all bad. For example, if you are a young male interested in being preyed upon by what is commonly referred to today as the cougar (a horny, older woman aiming to mature a young man—sexually), then there is a website that was created several years ago meant to suit your needs. That website is called UrbanCougar.com.

UrbanCougar.com was built with three main purposes in mind: (1) to help young men track down "Cougar Dens," (2) to educate young men on the various classifications of the cougar so they can better prepare before they go hunting, and (3) to write about their hilarious encounter(s) the next day. If you are a young man looking to fulfill those three goals, I must caution you. Though I haven't been on the site for a long time (at least five years), it was pretty spot-on with the cougar dens in Los Angeles and very disappointing in its ability to locate cougar dens in Seattle (two cities where I previously lived). In the four years I lived in Seattle, I never found one.

Though I'd like to say that I am a brave soul that tamed many cougars in my day, I did not. From afar, the cougar is a beautiful, seemingly approachable animal. However, up close, it is a terrifying beast that can tear any young man to shreds. I hope that doesn't deter other young men from trying. If you have the courage, be sure to use UrbanCougar.com as a guidebook. (And, no ... UrbanCougar.com has not paid for advertising space in this book—although that's not a bad idea to consider.)

TWENTY SEVEN

Youtube: In Case You Never Have Anything Better To Do … Ever

We have reached the point in the book where we have moved past most of the conversations about meeting or connecting or locating people through websites or mobile applications. Now we're into the section of the book that I like to call, "Videos, Games, and Other Silly Shit I'd Like to Rant About!" Where better to start this section of the book than with YouTube …

I am going to say it because I think someone has to: YouTube is the biggest time waster that exists in the world today. I say that with some remorse knowing that I am as guilty as the next person in wasting way too much time using it.

Everyone loves to watch motion pictures. If you deny this, you, my friend (have we reached that point in our relationship?), are clearly a liar! Our obsession with motion pictures started with movies in the late 1800s, evolved with television, cable television, video cassettes, and eventually DVDs. Today, video on the Internet (both on smart phones and computers), at your fingertips, on demand has pushed us to the motion picture's pinnacle. The only (totally unimaginable) next step for motion picture watching would be to download motion pictures directly into your brain. (I would not be surprised if this actually happens one day.)

Videos today can range from a 10-second clip of your friend getting kicked in the nuts to a full-length motion picture or documentary. Everything can be uploaded and everything can be downloaded; YouTube sits at the center of it all. You might ask, "What about Netflix?" Kudos ... good point. Netflix holds a solid place in the marketplace, but they don't bring you every form of video known to man like YouTube (more to come in chapter 28 about this). Television shows and movies, which can be downloaded from Netflix, are more of a commitment than a one-minute clip of a guy screaming about a double rainbow. Netflix is also not free. Plus, Netflix is blocked on my company's web server. Therefore, I can't watch Netflix during the day, which makes it much less of a time waster (but also makes it way less awesome than YouTube in terms of awesomeness!).

The biggest problem with YouTube is that it is always more exciting than what you are doing at any given moment. Let's test this theory. Later on when you are playing chess with your brother, take a break, go onto YouTube, and type in "chess brother." I guarantee there will be a video of two brothers playing chess with life-size pieces. Now the game you were just playing seems super boring by comparison. When you are off playing basketball with some friends, pull out your phone, go onto YouTube, and type in "basketball shot." You'll probably get directed to a video of some 12-year-old kid hitting a full-court shot ... something you will NEVER do. The next time you're in the missionary position with your significant other, call timeout for a bathroom break, sneak over to the computer, and type in "sex," just plain, old "sex"! After watching 20 seconds of other people having sex, your intuition will be confirmed that yes, you are horrific at sex. At this point, you'll quietly climb out the window and run far, far away, too embarrassed to ever show your face amongst normal people again, and join an abstinence cult (like the Catholic Church).

THE DEATH OF HUMAN INTERACTION

Despite my feelings about YouTube, it is here to stay. And, if it wasn't YouTube, it'd be something else. I just wish people found more interesting things in their life to talk about than YouTube videos. In this regard, YouTube is almost the bane to our society that reality television is (more about this in "I HATE Reality Television and So Should You"). One of my biggest pet peeves is when you go to hang out with some friends and one of them cracks out a computer or an iPhone to show everyone a video clip they found the other day of a dog peeing on his owner or a turtle dancing to the alphabet song. I'd rather be present, watching the dog pee on his owner, so that I could then laugh in his face. Call me mean, but half the fun in that scenario is laughing in the guy's face.

A common message in this book is that there is something to be said about interacting with the people directly in front of you by living in the moment. When we let mediums such as YouTube get in between us, we're no longer in the game, we're no longer making memories; instead, we're simply watching others from the sidelines.

Don't get me wrong; entertainment is one of the greatest assets in our society. It is a wonderful thing to be amused, to laugh, to cry. And there are so many gifted people out there that have the ability to play with our emotions, to make us feel ... just plain, old feel. Those people deserve a medium such as YouTube in order to shine. For them, YouTube provides a world of accessibility to reach viewers in a fashion different from what has ever been available to them. Therefore, it is up to viewers to watch responsibly.

After this book is published, if anyone from my office happens to read this, they might call me a hypocrite. I will wear that title with pride because I do abuse YouTube in the office setting. I listen to music videos (which wouldn't be the case if my company hadn't blocked Pandora ... seriously, what the hell?). I watch political commentary, speeches, and debates. (I'm one step beyond a political junkie ... probably more a political whore.) I even occasionally (but not often) go one step too far by watching clips from television shows or movies. I'm not a bad person, but yes, I am a hypocrite. Aren't we all?

I think what we need, perhaps even fed through YouTube channels (go right to the source), is a campaign suggesting that we watch responsibly, something similar to the "Drink Responsibly" ads flooding our televisions—which appear to be targeted at male audiences as they generally air during televised sporting events. What are they implying? It's funny that we even have to suggest to teenage and adult men and women to be responsible, but without that message, people don't know the difference between responsibility and the lack thereof. (I honestly believe there are many people out there who don't realize that something as basic as watching porn on their computer—via YouTube or some other means—is irresponsible and someone must instruct them as such.)

As a face for this campaign, we should recruit many of the dumbass YouTube celebrities like Rebecca Black. I'm sure, in Rebecca's case, she'd love to be paid to tell people to watch responsibly and, accordingly, to not view her videos. This would be a much more sensible business decision than having her pull her made-for-YouTube music video off the site altogether due to embarrassment. (If you are going to post a public video of yourself on YouTube, I feel no sympathy for the embarrassment you feel when people watch it and make fun of you for it. It's what you asked for!) YouTube (or whoever administered the campaign) would also probably pay her better than the advertising money she was probably making from her music video. It'd be a win-win; she'd get the fame and fortune she's after and people would no longer accidentally suffer through the worst music video of all time!

For now, until the day of the "Watch Responsibly" campaign, you're going to have to get that message through this chapter (which happens to be buried deep within this book).

THE DEATH OF HUMAN INTERACTION

YouTube, despite my harsh comments, please do not restrict my access to your site. I just don't know how I could possibly fill up my days without you. I don't remember the world before you and I can't imagine a world without you, especially since my Netflix is blocked at work and, due to licensing issues, their video streaming options have gone to shit in recent years.

TWENTY EIGHT

Netflix And Hulu: Perhaps Tooooo Easy

I should inform you that when I originally wrote this chapter, it was during a time that Netflix seemed to have better programming and before I streamed Hulu Plus through the Roku attached to my television. In this chapter, I sing some praise to these services; those services, over the past couple years, have been entertaining in a sense that they fill a void (I no longer subscribe to cable television), but they are quite disappointing.

Once upon a time, Aaron Panzer graced the classrooms of the S.I. Newhouse School of Public Communications at Syracuse University. A very diligent student (occasionally, when he wasn't playing or watching endless amounts of basketball), Aaron majored in "Television, Radio, Film" as any recovering television addict obviously would. At Syracuse, Aaron learned the art of television and film production (honestly, who cares about radio these days?) and storytelling. He took time to understand the challenges associated with taking a story idea, developing it into a well-designed script, and producing a video. To say the least, it takes endless hours of critical thinking, hard work, tears, and agony to get to the point where you have a final product worthy of showing anyone, something you are proud of. It takes time, creativity, and skills to reach that finish line. It is an EXTREMELY difficult accomplishment.

The reason I tell you this is three-fold: (1) to stress the point that it is so easy to produce a video (using your home camcorder or computer camera) that is absolute crap, that has no story and no point, and that you can upload in a matter of minutes onto a site like YouTube; (2) to emphasize that professionally developed reality television is not much better (from a creative and production standpoint) than what I described in my previous point; (3) to communicate that most of the traditional television and movie programming offered to viewers through mediums like Netflix and Hulu is okay by me.

Yes, few times throughout this book will you see the phrase "okay by me" when it comes to a popular technology in this day and age. Netflix and Hulu both are companies that I have respect for in terms of the quality of the programs/content they offer to their viewers. Having worked in Hollywood in a previous life, I strongly respect what it takes to make something that requires brainstorming/drafting out an idea, writing dialogue, arranging for production, shooting a video, and editing a video in a cohesive fashion that not only makes sense in the end, but is also entertaining. No … my problem with Netflix and Hulu is not with what they offer; instead, my problem with these two companies (and ones similar) is the implications attached to how their product(s) is offered.

Netflix, which once upon a time (approximately five years ago) was solely a mail-order service, now offers its customers the opportunity to be instantly entertained from a selection of hundreds of movies and television programs on their computer or through their video game systems for a simple fee of less than $10 a month. Hulu goes one step farther; though their selection of programming is not as impressive as what you'll find at Netflix, they offer their basic service completely free of charge. Essentially, what companies like Netflix and Hulu have done is torn down the barriers viewers used to face when wanting to watch television or movies.

THE DEATH OF HUMAN INTERACTION

Coupled with the fact that today most households have at least one computer and access to high-speed Internet, because of the services offered by Netflix and Hulu, people no longer need to buy a DVD or VHS player to watch movies; they no longer need to go to the video store and pay three to five dollars to rent one movie for two days; they no longer need to use a DVR or a VHS to record television programs they won't have time to watch when they originally air; they no longer need to order *TV Guide* to know when their favorite programs are airing, etc. Using these services, people can save a substantial amount of time and money. Isn't that wonderful?

No, not a bit. Let's be honest with ourselves. (If we're not, who else will be?) When given the opportunity, most of us in today's world prefer the path of laziness. It's not the appeal of laziness that drives us there; it's the fact that laziness is generally easy (or easier); it's the path of least resistance. At the end of each work day, we tell ourselves, "I use my brain all day at work," "I worked hard all day; I just want to veg out," "I'm tired," to convince ourselves that we have already challenged ourselves enough for the day and no longer need to be challenged any further until tomorrow. But why is that? Why do we give up five to seven hours, five days a week (which translates into countless hours a year) to the excuse that we no longer need to use or stretch our brains in any given way once the work day ends? It's because of choice.

Nine times out of 10, most of us prefer to choose the easy path over the hard path. We prefer to dial back brain usage by watching a video on Netflix or Hulu as opposed to opening up a book; after all, opening up a book means reading, comprehending, and painting pictures with our imagination. That is SOOO much more work for our brains than turning on a television show and allowing the screen in front of us to do all that for us.

Netflix and Hulu are not wonderful. When we are faced with the choice of easy vs. hard, we choose easy, which translates into laziness.

Services like Netflix and Hulu make it easier for us to stay in on a Wednesday night as opposed to braving a cold winter night to attend a poetry reading with friends at a coffee shop, a trivia night at a local pub, or to go to a park to play basketball or soccer. With each passing year and every new technology, it is becoming tougher for us to continue to be social (sometimes in the traditional sense or, in the case of Netflix and Hulu, at all). Most of us don't want tougher. Most of us desire Netflix and Hulu.

On top of this, I think the most tragic effect Netflix has had (more so than Hulu) is one that no one even acknowledges: Due to the impact that Netflix has had on traditional video stores, forcing them to become unprofitable and having to close their doors, there are no longer back rooms for customers wearing trench coats, sunglasses, and hats to walk into to search for good porn to beat off to that night.

Being a kid that grew up in the '80s and '90s, I often asked myself what that back room was where that mysteriously dressed-up man walked into during the '80s, and then I laughed hard at him when I better understood what he was after during the '90s. (Now I just envy him as I will never have a chance to be that man myself.)

And, as a high schooler in the late '90s, my friends and I used to love to sneak into that room just to see the large naked boobs on the VHS (yes, VHS) covers while discovering that most of the men costumed up in trench coats were my teachers and sports coaches. (I would probably say that it was more awkward for them than us on those occasions.)

Because of Netflix (I blame you entirely Netflix), my children won't be able to experience the same curious and humorous opportunities that I had. The porn room is something they will never understand; their lives will be less fulfilled because of it. (I'd also say they won't have the opportunity to sneak in good porn as a teenager, but with

THE DEATH OF HUMAN INTERACTION

the Internet, that certainly won't be the case. However, they'll have to be smart about getting through my Fort Knox-style security parental controls I will put into place.)

Netflix and Hulu have certainly had their negative impacts on society, but they are not one of the worst things I discuss in this book.

TWENTY NINE

I Hate Reality Television And So Should You

I apologize up front for the tone of this chapter. More so in this chapter than any other do I proceed to lecture as opposed to share thoughts, stories, and insights. But, in my defense, this chapter is about something absolutely terrible: reality television.

I hate reality television. Actually, "hate" might be too strong of a word. Nope, not in this case.

I hate reality television. I, like the rest of you suckers out there, have succumbed numerous times to watching a show filled with the drama (some staged, some real) of other people's lives—people I've never met, never want to meet, and personally would feel no remorse for if they ceased to exist (in TV land ... come on, I'm not entirely coldhearted). These are ordinary people much like you and me that television producers one day decided would be interesting to follow around. It all started with *The Real World* on MTV, then *Road Rules*, and eventually moved on to every single broadcast and cable network you've heard of (and many you've never heard of) due to the success of *Survivor* on CBS. (Thank you, Mark Burnett!)

Mom, Dad, and the five other readers of this book ... stop watching reality television! Stop encouraging these entertainment hacks.

Somehow we have all been duped. One day, a group of supervillains seeking world domination concocted the most evil, genius plan in the history of supervillainry. They determined that if they dumbed down all mankind to an intelligence level just above that of a lemming, they could use mind control tactics in their pursuit. So they created reality television. The problem they never considered was how powerful their innovation would become. As they began flipping through the channels one Monday evening, determined not to settle on another rerun of *Chuck*, they caught an episode of *Dancing with the Stars* and unsuspectingly fell into their own trap.

I get that our society thrives on drama. After all, drama is interesting to watch whether it is incorporated into our lives or the lives of others. But when you watch reality television, all you are doing is watching the lives of other people as opposed to experiencing life for yourself. Don't tell me you're not as bad as most people, that your reality TV rotation simply consists of an hour of *The Bachelor* or *American Idol* each week—that's all.

I know you because I know my coworkers, whether it was the 40-year-old music manager, 23-year-old administrative assistant at the advertising agency, or 60-year-old engineer at the utility company, everyone has their guilty pleasures. And no one wants to be alone with their guilty pleasures, so they go to work the next day and have numerous conversations, determined to talk to anyone who will listen. They'll mention how "Simon is such a jerk" because of the way he kicked some "untalented bum" off the show this week. I have been on the receiving end of that conversation more times than I can count (and occasionally on the giving end); I don't like it.

I don't like it because at the end of the conversation, I always have to ask the same question, "Who the hell is Simon?" If I become VERY curious, then I have to go online to research who Simon is, what he said, and why he kicked that so-called "untalented bum" off his television

THE DEATH OF HUMAN INTERACTION

program (remember that I have OCD). At that point, *American Idol* has taken up way more than an hour of my coworker's time; plus, it has also wasted an uncalculated amount of my time. And my coworker hasn't yet had a chance to call all his or her friends to discuss the whole thing after work. I'd pity his/her friends if I hadn't just endured the same torture. (Next time just waterboard me!)

At some point, you have to ask yourself, "Why? Why the hell am I watching train wreck after train wreck?" Well, there are ways to avoid it or free yourself from the reality television trap. (I cannot offer a 100 percent guarantee that the following will allow you to successfully cut reality television entirely out of your life. After all, there is such a thing as human error.) These include:

1. Climb to the top of a very tall building with your television in tow. Once you reach the roof, throw it as far and as hard as you can.
   (This might not be the most recommended option as it could lead to some jail time depending on who sees you throw it and if it hits anyone. If it does hit someone, they were probably on their cell phone instead of paying attention to the world around them; in that case, they probably deserved it.)
2. Throw your television in the trash.
   (Or if you want to be a good environmental steward, recycle or donate it—although, donating it could lead to a similar fate for the next purchaser—sucker!)
3. Bury your television set in a deep hole in the backyard.
   (This could have negative environmental consequences similar to #2. Alternatively, it could grow into a tree that produces new TVs like fruit, which could lead to a lucrative electronics business, assuming they are high-definition flat screens. Who actually buys a non-HD TV these days?)
4. If any of the previous suggestions fail you, unplug it or turn the damn television off!

(Or ask someone else to do this for you if you don't know how to operate a power cord. And take the batteries out of your remote just for good measure.)
5. Avoid channels that air reality television programming.
(This unfortunately will leave you to watch only CSPAN and CSPAN 2, which to some extent can also be considered reality television—the most excruciatingly boring kind of it!)
6. Shun your coworkers when they try to speak with you about the show they watched last night.
The problems you may run into here include:
   a. You will come off as an antisocial jackass to your coworkers, which, depending on your office environment, could lead to something as traumatic as a tarring and feathering (assuming your coworkers prefer using colonial torture methods).
   b. You may have to rely on other facets of society that are further enhancing the death of human interaction, such as ignoring people right in front of you by using your cell phone, Blackberry, or computer. In this case, it is a sacrifice I believe you should make because, as I have already mentioned, I HATE reality television and you should too.
3. Pretend you're autistic.
(This one is just wrong, but hey, if you can pull it off with a straight face day after day with no remorse, more power to you—you sick son of a bitch!)

Perhaps I should apologize to you; throughout this chapter, I have been a little hard on you. After all, if you're reading this book, reality television hasn't entirely taken over your life. Plus, as I previously conceded, I too succumbed to the "Devil." That is the terrible truth that fuels my fire.

I am an avid watcher of shows like *The Biggest Loser* and *The Apprentice*. (Well, I used to be before Trump demonstrated over the past few years that he is an even bigger douche-bag than we originally thought—can

THE DEATH OF HUMAN INTERACTION

I see your birth certificate?) I wish I had a good excuse for myself. (Wait ... this is my book. I have control. I can tell you whatever I want and you have to believe it.) At least the two shows I watch have redeeming qualities that ones you watch do not. (No, no they don't. Aaron, it's time to save face.) Still, much like you, I tend to ask myself at the end of each episode, "What happened to the past two hours?" "What the hell did I just watch?" "Why am I crying?" and "Are there any more Kleenex?" Then, I step into my secret laboratory and plot my revenge against the crafty Mark Burnett (both for the hours of my life he stole watching his shows and the hours I spent plotting my revenge).

While I am frustrated and angered over reality television, I must admit some shows do have certain redeeming qualities (yes, again with the "redeeming qualities" bullshit). For example, *The Contender*, another show I used to watch, showcased the talents of some gritty boxers that fought through the years to get their one chance to prove their abilities in a *Rocky*-esque manner. (*Coincidentally* it was produced by Sylvester Stallone.) *The Contender* taught people to never give up because if you work hard, your dreams may come true. A show like the *The Biggest Loser* also has a positive impact, teaching people how to take control of their lives, eat better, exercise, and ultimately, proving that anyone can become healthy if they truly want it. And a show like *Joe Millionaire* taught men how to lie straight through their teeth to women. (Never mind ... this one might not be the best example.)

For a moment, upon reflection of the aforementioned redeeming qualities, I think that maybe reality television does have a purpose in pushing this world forward toward goodness; maybe it's more than just an overpowering tabloid directly fed into your home seven days a week.

Then I remember shows like *John and Kate Plus Eight*. I am proud to say I never watched this show or bought into all the subsequent drama. As a nonviewer, I can tell you what I learned from this show is that if you procreate enough, you can have your own television show leading to fame and fortune. Since when is having swimming sperm, fertile eggs, and the inability to use birth control a talent to be celebrated? Why was this entire country so obsessed with this couple, their eight children, and their common breakup of "husband cheats on wife so wife divorces husband"?

I remember one time walking by a row of televisions in an airport when John and his lawyer were on *Larry King Live* discussing the divorce. I stopped to watch for three minutes, all the while thinking to myself, "Is this really newsworthy? There had to have been some bombing, coup, or 'act of terrorism' in some developing country somewhere in the world that should take precedence over this topic. (I hesitate to call it a 'news story')." Were there no wildfires, earthquakes, epidemic outbreaks, or genocides in the world that could have preempted that story that day? I would have even been fine with a story about the discovery of a bomb within the past 30 minutes in the airport I happened to be standing in at that very moment over John and Kate. I'm not typically so morbid, but COME ON ... REALLY?

The "John and Kate" topic of discussion, all created by reality television, was sadly inescapable. It was a media circus that validated the idea that the world wanted subsequent media circuses surrounding people like Tiger Woods or Charlie Sheen (who actually have legitimate reasons for being famous).

Well, allow me to invalidate that notion. We don't want that media circus! We're sick of seeing and hearing it! Charlie Sheen is drugged up, cheating on his wife, and screaming anti-Semitic remarks at his producer. Where is the news story? Hasn't some of Charlie Sheen's appeal always been that he sits somewhere between "dumbass" and "fuck up?" I could have told you all the same things about him in the mid-1980s. There is no current event. But TV news producers convince you that one exists in order to build ratings.

(As an aside, Charlie is still on my list of top five celebrities to have a beer with. Can you imagine walking away from that conversation having either laughed your ass off or possessing your very own mug shot to show your grandkids one day? My only hope is that he doesn't die before I get a chance to live out that dream.)

Anyway, getting back to John and Kate (it is so easy to go off on Charlie Sheen tangents!), perhaps I'm being too hard on John and Kate. After all, they didn't ask for the media circus. Right? ACTUALLY, they did. They asked for it the minute that they signed a contract to have their own reality television show exposing their entire existence. The thing that probably isn't fair is blaming them for igniting the troubled-marriage media circus trend. But if not them, who is to blame?

Two words ... Slick Willy! President Clinton's "untimely affair" created the biggest media circus of its kind. The utter frenzy and the sky-high ratings that ensued from this breaking news convinced television producers that people want to hear all the "he-said, she-said, let's look at this situation from a million different angles while allowing so-called experts to chime in" bullshit. We didn't and we don't. All we really care(d) about is how is this going to impact our lives? Is Al Gore moving to the Oval Office? What types of cigars did he use? (If the answer was Cuban, subsequent questions would have naturally followed given the trade embargo.)

I admit that I have a very cynical opinion of reality television, but I promise you that the more you think about the content, the messages, the people, and the nature of these shows, you too will move to a similar line of thought. When you look at the dirty truth, it is difficult to deny my line of thought unless what you want is to believe a lie. It is simple to understand the worthlessness that is reality television. However, most people choose to watch it because it is easy to believe it offers value.

Despite the title and message of this chapter, if any producers of the Amazing Race *ever happen to read this book, please consider me as a future contestant on your show.*

THIRTY

Erica Rose Proves My Point

This is an addendum to chapter 31. It further proves my point about reality TV!

Since completing the chapter "I HATE Reality Television and So Should You," I discovered that I know someone from years past that became a reality television *star*. Erica Rose, a contestant on the ninth season of *The Bachelor* and possibly the most controversial woman to ever be on the show, interned with me at Spyglass Entertainment during the summer of 2003.

Erica struck me as a bit different from the very beginning. Within the first five minutes of meeting her, she informed me, without inquiry, that her father is the top breast doctor in all of Houston, her breasts are real, and so are her mother's. To make her feel more comfortable, I politely replied that mine are also real.

That is the type of person that Erica is—very direct, a quality I do appreciate in people. However, the problem with Erica's directness is that it comes without any level of discretion, a lesson I learned fairly quickly. For example, I was okay with her telling me that she thought I was cute, that she enjoyed the fact that I am Jewish (as is she), and that she wanted to fornicate with me. I didn't quite appreciate her directness, however, when she told the other five interns we worked with as well as a handful of my friends that I was a virgin at the time. I suppose she didn't appreciate my reciprocal directness when I politely declined her offer for sex. (How could I have accepted considering she smokes? What would my mother have said? And yes, I was a virgin until I was 21, but that's a story for another time ... YAY ABSTINANCE!) Other examples of her directness included telling the entire group of interns that (1) the girl from Michigan was lame and boring, (2) the guy from Michigan was a "tool" because he had a crush on the girl from Michigan, and (3) the girl from Harvard was a lesbian.

In life, there are some people that you are sad to say "good-bye" to after spending a considerable amount of time with them. Erica Rose was not one of them. I was happy to delete her from my cell phone contact list and from my life.

A few years later, I ran into Erica at a mutual friend's event in Los Angeles. Call me traditional, but when I bump into someone I haven't seen in a while, even if that person is Erica Rose, I stop to catch up with them. In the short conversation we had, Erica first acted like she hardly remembered me. Then, before moving on to torture the next poor soul, she explained that she was "THE star of this season's *The Bachelor*." I cared about this almost as much as I cared about the Teletubbies ... not just because *I HATE Reality Television and So Should You*, but it was *The Bachelor*. How many single, straight guys do you know that actually watch that show? Anyway, I digress ...

Flash forward to today. As I finished writing chapter 29, I asked myself, "Whatever happened to Erica Rose?" (a question I am certain most of you have asked yourself at some point in your life). So I turned to my old friend (or enemy), the World Wide Web. I was able to find clips of Erica Rose on YouTube. What I learned is that the Erica Rose that offended every single intern at Spyglass Entertainment during the summer of 2003 successfully did the same to every single cast member on the ninth season of *The Bachelor*—people hated her. When I asked my friends who religiously watch *The Bachelor* if they remembered her,

THE DEATH OF HUMAN INTERACTION

they replied, "Oh my gosh, you know Erica Rose! She's the worst person ever on that show … EVER! [I may have added that last "EVER!" for effect.] Watching her was like watching a train wreck." Apparently, Erica Rose was compelling.

I HATE Reality Television and So Should You because of people like Erica Rose. Erica comes from a very rich family; she was born into a life filled with opportunity. She could have gone to school to become a neurosurgeon (well, maybe not a neurosurgeon … she is actually a very smart girl—just not neurosurgeon smart). Because of her financial freedom she could have spent the majority of her time volunteering. She could have spent more time giving back to the world that gave her so much from the very beginning. But, alas, Erica Rose has always been focused on herself. Erica Rose has also always been determined to stir up drama. Erica Rose has always been interested in gaining the fame of a C-rate Paris Hilton (which would make her a G-rate celebrity?). And we, through the medium (reality television), glorify a person like Erica Rose.

I will say she does offer entertainment—cheap, dirty entertainment, like when you leave an Atlantic City strip club at three in the morning (not that I've ever done that … in the past 10 years). You got lost in the show while it lasted, but immediately sought lighter fluid to burn your entire body—starting with your eyes—directly afterwards.

Erica Rose is pound-for-pound, one of the worst human beings I have ever gotten the chance to know. With that said, why do we glorify her? Why do we allow ourselves to get caught up in the hoopla that is she? Why did VH1 recently put her on a new show called *You're Cut Off*? Why? Why? Why? Why? Why?

Reality TV, I hate you so much!

THIRTY ONE

Information Overload 1.0

If you haven't picked up on my dissatisfaction with reality TV by now, you probably never will. Reality TV, though, is not the only form of entertainment that dominates our time and attention. There is something else that, in its purest form, is not actually meant to be entertainment. But when ratings and advertising dollars are brought into the equation, this "something" becomes an obnoxious form of entertainment that I wish we were not subjected to.

I have something to tell you that is a bit difficult for me. It is not difficult because it is something dark and deep, morbid, or embarrassing. It is not difficult because I care about the general focal point I am about to attack. It is difficult because I need to relay my message in a sound enough manner that you understand my points (and perhaps laugh at all the hilarious sarcasm) while not offending my beautiful, sweet, kindhearted, forgiving wife whose industry (however, not necessarily her role in it) is one of the banes of my existence.

You see, my wife is a local news reporter and has been for going on six years. She works hard doing what she loves, and she loves it because, to her, providing the public with unbiased news and information is socially important. I agree with her as I've seen her present stories regarding EBT card scams, police corruption, and racially motivated violence. She generally creates one or two, one- to four-minute news stories per day that stick to the facts and just the facts. It is her obligation to deliver the truth about whatever situation she is reporting without any editorializing. I love the work she does and her passion toward it. I have almost no problem with the output of most local television news broadcasts nationwide. What I do have a problem with are their cousins in the cable world! (I do admit there is no direct correlation between the theme of this book and 24/7 news programming. However, I believe it is an area worth exploring because it is something that has had a major impact on all our behaviors.)

There are three 24/7 cable *news* channels (or so they call themselves) that exist in the United States: Fox News, MSNBC, and CNN. Each one has its individual identity that has demonstrated a horrific impact on society (which I will get to in a moment). Together, they also share common traits that have done more harm than good. For example, 24/7 news was the first avenue we all traveled down toward information overload in this country. This forum came into place before the Internet became wildly popular, making the mistake of assuming there is actually enough news that happens in one day to run programming infinitely.

I heard one time that when CBS moved from the 15-minute news format to the 30-minute news format, Walter Cronkite asked something along the lines of, "What the hell am I supposed to talk about for the other 15 minutes?" What he was suggesting was that there is not a significant amount of real news that actually occurs in one average day. The news, the REAL news (meaning facts and such), can be told within 15 minutes. The rest is just filling time. I absolutely agree with Cronkite (especially if that is what he meant … which he must have or else I wouldn't have suggested it in this completely factual book), which leads me to the thought that it is extremely audacious for an organization to create what they call a 24/7 *NEWS* channel. How can anyone possibly suggest that they can fill 24/7 television programming with relevant news and information when Cronkite had a difficult time moving from a 15- to 30-minute format?

THE DEATH OF HUMAN INTERACTION

The answer is they can't and they don't. They realized this long ago and have been more focused on ratings and selling advertising than delivering hard-hitting, relevant, unbiased news stories to their viewers. The news channels tend to stretch out the biggest stories of the day and add anywhere from five minutes to three hours' worth of editorial commentary into their broadcasts, essentially turning relevant news stories into magazine banter.

The lesser stories of the day, the ones that 30-40 years ago would not have gotten any national coverage and minimal local/regional coverage, are now getting serious air time. The *news* channels view them as filler, not giving a second thought to the fact that they are exposing people to stories that don't matter, not caring that they are giving those irrelevant stories some worthiness just because they were included. Essentially, instead of guiding their viewers in a positive direction and relaying the important news of the day, 24/7 *news* channels have blurred their messaging. Viewers no longer know what is relevant and what is not. They no longer know who is credible and who is not. Instead, viewers align themselves with personalities with whom they feel connected. They fall into a trap.

When it comes to implementing the deceitful, irresponsible strategy I have outlined above, no one is better at the game than Fox News (with MSNBC as runner-up and CNN coming in dead last). I could go on and on and on and on and on and on and on for hours and hours about what I hate about all three channels; I'll save you the long-winded rant. After all, everyone already knows that Fox News is so right-wing biased that they never grew a left-wing (probably *God's* fault as some FN correspondents might describe it) and have been aimlessly flying over Middle America for 15 years. MSNBC is so left-wing biased that they're hiring more intelligent personnel that happen to be worse at delivering a message than their Fox News counterparts. (Sound familiar? It's pretty much like a Democrat and Republican sparring in a political campaign. The only hope the Democrat has is that his audience is intelligent enough to comprehend his/her campaign messages.) CNN is so, well ... CNN is ... CNN was the first. CNN was the first, and now (according to the ratings) it is the worst. I hate 24/7 news with a complete passion, but I will say that I respect CNN because they are at least trying to stay a little more central (not necessarily unbiased as they clearing lean left), which has come to bite them in the ass. Regardless of their attempt to stay central, there are still 24 hours in the day and so much programming they have to fill that they have no choice but to editorialize the news. To that point, they are just as bad as their peers.

It is a fact that 99.9 percent of all Americans are absolutely 100 percent gullible. (Okay, it is possible that is my opinion and not a fact. Or is it?) The thing I hate most about 24/7 *news* channels is that they take advantage of people's gullibility. People are so gullible that they will trust anyone identified as a host or an expert on any television program. It doesn't matter if it is Caroline Rhea hosting *The Biggest Loser* (when she used to be the host), giving America tips on how to be healthy when she clearly looked like she was eating twelve Snickers bars every time she walked back into her trailer or LeVar Burton (the blind guy from *Star Trek: The Next Generation*) teaching kids how to read on his show *Reading Rainbow*. (Okay, I know he was playing a blind character and wasn't actually blind. Or was he?)

The Bill O'Reillys and Rachel Maddows of the world are equally irresponsible. I don't care if neither of them views his or her own show as an actual news program. The simple fact that they air their respective shows on channels that identify themselves as 24/7 *news* channels and don't specifically advertise their shows as magazine shows is misleading. The overarching purpose of news television is to deliver important, truthful, unbiased information to all its viewers. From 1980—when CNN originally launched—until now, news television (particularly on cable programming) has lost its focus on that purpose and has done a disservice to the people that rely on it. And it's not like the people behind the programming don't know what they're doing.

THE DEATH OF HUMAN INTERACTION

A few years ago, NBC finally grew a conscience and replaced Carolina Rhea on *The Biggest Loser* with Alison Sweeney, a host that actually resembles what a healthy person should look like (despite her plastic surgery). *News* channels (that's right, I'm talking to you Fox News, MSNBC, and CNN), you should be responsible with your obligation to the gullible saps across the country as well.

I'm sorry if I offended you and your profession, baby, but you and the other four readers of this book have to know the truth!

THIRTY TWO

Video Gaming Addiciton ... Perhaps?

Throughout this book I have discussed many forms of addiction—TV in general, Facebook, cell phones, cougar dens, reality TV—but none might be as addictive as video games, which is not to say they are the worst means of the death of human interaction (it's still pretty bad though).

What would be the point in writing this book, how could I honestly convey thoughts, beliefs, ideas, etc. to you, if I was not honest with you (hombre a hombre o hombre a mujer) throughout? To this point in this book, I have disclosed my "former" addictions, including television, Facebook, and YouTube (occasionally not-so-former addictions when I relapse). But the one I have yet to mention, which I still hesitate to, is my sheer addiction to video games. As if this was our first date, I hesitated to tell you about this addiction because I didn't want you to get the wrong impression, Baby. (Is it too soon to call you "Baby?") I didn't want you to think of me as a nerd that plays fantasy or war games, like *Halo 3* or *Call of Duty*. (And yes, I did play *Legend of Zelda* growing up, but who didn't? Don't even try to judge me on that.) No, no, no ... I am not that type of video game addict; I am a WAY cooler video game addict. The types of video games that I am easily addicted to include: (1) sports video games (macho, of course), (2) bar video games (yeah, I like to party), and (3) mobile video games. (Well,

I have no excuse other than that they just happen to be there in the palm of my hand ready to be used at any given moment.)

Sports Video Games

Saying that I love sports video games is too broad; there are absolutely no specifics to paint you a picture. Bear with me as I take you through some of the evolution of video games and video game systems to where we are today.

When I was five years old, my parents bought my brothers and me our first Nintendo. (You might ask, "First? That implies you had more than one Nintendo." Sadly, that is the case. But that is a story for later in the chapter ... perhaps section two.) Prior to the Nintendo, we owned an Atari that, in itself, was an incredible machine; however, Nintendo absolutely blew it out of the water! For example, Atari had the game *Mario Brothers* and Nintendo had the game *Super Mario Brothers*. (You see what I mean?) But even more than the difference between *Super* and regular *Mario Brothers*, Nintendo brought with it a large array of games to choose from. Atari brought video games from the arcade to the living room. Nintendo opened up a world of options—one of which was sports video games.

From ages five to 10, I fell in love with games such as *RBI Baseball, Double Dribble, Mike Tyson's Punch-Out!!, Tennis* (Have you ever heard of any other game with such a simple name?), *Ice Hockey* (I suppose you have), and *Bases Loaded*. But the best of them all (still, in my opinion, the greatest sports video game and probably the best video game ever invented) was *Tecmo Bowl*. (I do not know nor have I ever known where the name "Tecmo" comes from, but who the hell cares! Like I said, it is the best game ever!) If you played *Tecmo Bowl* growing up, you know exactly what I mean. You know as well as I do that Bo Jackson is the best running back in the game, Lawrence Taylor is the best defensive player, and the 49ers is the best team. And, even though there are only four plays to choose from, the graphics are terrible, and everything is

THE DEATH OF HUMAN INTERACTION

so damn predictable, I would take that game over any EA Sports game developed today. If you grew up after *Tecmo Bowl* was a huge hit, you were seriously deprived.

Whether it was my brother and I or my friends and I, it was always a blast competing with one another in a sports arena that didn't actually require us to walk out of the house into the sun where there was fresh air. ("Was" is the key word, but we'll discuss that more in a future book that I pen regarding global warming. You'll find it on the bookshelves in 2023 if humans still exist.) We never had to work up a sweat, we never had to shower before dinner, and we never had to dirty our clothes (a bonus for my mom). We also had the option of playing any sport we wanted at any time, and we were not the least bit dependent on weather or number of players. Hell, even if you were all alone (as I often was, especially after I discovered video games and realized I didn't need any friends), you could still play against the computer (a nonhuman machine, as I understood it, was the only friend I needed). It was magnificent; for a sports addict like me, I had sports any and all of the time!

Some may call this sort of addiction sad. Alright, fine! You'd be right. (Get off my case!) But for a competition addict (another type of addiction I didn't really cover in this book) like me, something that supported my need and that sat in my basement ready for use 24/7, was … magical!

As I got older and the games became more lifelike, the addiction only grew stronger. Through the '90s, I played games on Super Nintendo and Nintendo 64. Then, in the earlier part of last decade came the greatest advancement of all … the Sega Dreamcast. With it came the introduction of the Sega Sports 2K series of games, which I consider to be the best series of sports video games today, especially the NBA 2K series. I mastered this series of video games to the point that I could demolish all my close friends, particularly the ones with whom I am most competitive. (Everyone has friends like that and should empathize with those sentiments.) Even as the Dreamcast disappeared and the Playstation, the Xbox, and Nintendo Wii took center stage, the 2K series lived on. And though I do not leave my Playstation hooked up anymore (in an effort to try to avoid the time waster), every so often when I play one of those friends in one those games, I still kick their ass and smile for days about it! (Upon rereading that last sentence, I've come to the conclusion that I possibly [probably] lead a sad existence.)

Bar Video Games

Anyone that says they don't enjoy bar video games is just a liar! This point is validated by the fact that when you are drinking, anything is fun (or more fun). Writing a biology term paper, talking with your best friend's very recent ex-girlfriend, talking with your own very recent ex-girlfriend, watching Fox News—all are more fun when you are drinking. (With the exception of the last one, which is never fun! It wouldn't even be fun if you were tripping off your ass and had no idea that you were watching Fox News, instead thinking you were watching Will Ferrell's movie *Anchorman.*) My point being, bar video games are fun for the whole family.

The thing is, however, video games at a bar can be as antisocial as video games anywhere else. Some video games have been designed to be a bit more social, like *Golden Tee* and *Big Buck Hunter*, which are essentially set up for two to four drunk bastards to go head-to-head for hours on end. The problem with these games is that someone always has to lose. When drinking, everything seems amplified, including losing. For example, the drunk version of any person would get way more pissed off than the sober version and is 900 percent more likely to ignore inhibitions, which usually leads to arguments that quickly escalate. Before they know it, as a result of *Golden Tee*, two to four friends get into a screaming match with one another that either leads to them storming off in separate directions or throwing fists at one another and getting kicked out of the bar. In either instance,

THE DEATH OF HUMAN INTERACTION

one person ends up hooking up with a mistake (to put it lightly), while one to three people get so shit-faced that they wake up in a McDonald's parking lot the next morning with sweet-and-sour sauce all over their face(s) and two to twenty half-eaten Chicken McNuggets on the ground next to them. (I have no idea why they eat only half a McNugget before moving on to the next one; nor do they.) Hence, multiplayer bar video games are not necessarily as social as they may seem. (I should point out that darts and/or billiards could prove to be a worse substitution for bar video games in the aforementioned scenario as the participating parties have a weapon in hand when playing either of these two bar games.) At best, the players are cordial and talkative strangers in the beginning and at separate ends of the bar sulking and drinking their pain away in the end. At worst, they are best friends in the beginning and, in the end, two are in jail (both with newly minted tramp stamps above their asses), one is now an expecting father, and the other bought a pet hyena that subsequently ripped his/her face off.

While less dangerous, the solo video games (which are my preference) are far from social. I'm speaking particularly about those touch-screen video games found at many bars. I can sit and play one of those machines for hours and forget what day of the week it is. The best of the games (or worst, considering the theme of this book) is the *Erotic Match Play* game. For those of you who have never played it, this game essentially involves staring at two almost identical photos of a mostly naked woman and determining the five differences between the two photos. If you find all the differences before time runs out, you move on to the next round to look at the next set of two photos of the next mostly naked woman. To summarize, you stare almost endlessly at mostly naked women in this game from beginning to end—the perfect bar game for any heterosexual man. (Oddly enough, there is also a choice to look at mostly naked men instead of women, but whenever I have played with women or homosexual men, they always prefer playing with the mostly naked women. I still haven't figured out why that is. If you know the answer, please send me a message via MySpace.)

Even when other people (friends or strangers) notice you playing the game (which happens all the time) and decide to join in, each person is still pretty much playing a game by themselves. This is because, in this scenario, there is no talking, no high fiving, no eye contact with one another; people simply jointly stare at the photos, determine the differences, point them out, and wait for the next round to start. *Erotic Match Play* is just about the most antisocial thing you can play in a typically social atmosphere; on a positive note, however, you are looking at pictures of mostly naked women.

Mobile Video Games

The worst of all the types of video games are mobile ones! I don't care if you play *Angry Birds, Brick Breaker, Sudoku,* or some sort of Scrabble-esque game, they are all very routine, basic, mind-numbing, and far too accessible. Let's take the last point first. The fact that these games can be found on your smart phone or notebook means that you have them at your disposal AT ALL TIMES (until your battery runs out and you discover your friend stole your charger because he lost his and didn't want to spend the money to buy a new one). This means that when sitting in a doctor's office (instead of reading a magazine), when riding the bus (instead of meeting someone new), when sitting in a coffee shop (instead of reading a book), when lounging in a park (instead of enjoying the surroundings), instead of expanding upon your horizons, you have the easy ability and (in this day and age) seemingly natural instinct to turn on your mobile phone and play a video game.

Points one through three above all relate to one another in the sense that the video games you will find on a mobile device are not as robust as those you will find on a physically larger gaming system. That means people (like me) get caught in the trap of playing the same simple games over and over again as if anything in the game will ever change or the challenges will ever get more difficult. In fact, the only thing that gets us to move on from this game is when a flight attendant tells us to power down our mobile device.

The issue to me is that smart phones and notebooks have too many capabilities and are too easy to take with you when you travel. They put people in the situation of having to choose *Angry Birds* over more basic, natural human sociological behaviors.

I have a solution to this problem, although I realize that it isn't complete. My solution is to slowly move people back to natural human sociological behaviors by first reintroducing them to the mobile gaming systems of the past while stripping them of the mobile gaming applications of the present on their smart phones. First, we could reintroduce the Gameboy Advance, followed by the original Game Boy, and eventually handheld poker and black jack games. We could get everyone hooked on the original *Tetris* (potentially the most addictive game ever), which would serve as the ultimate distraction while we rid the world of smart phone gaming applications. Then, when they don't even remember smart phone games or their obsession with them, we pull the Gameboys and handheld gambling games away.

I know it will be tough for several weeks. Many people will wake up at odd hours of the night in a complete sweat. There will be nightmares. There will be weight gain. There will be hair loss. In the end, the silicon nicotine will seep out of their veins and they (meaning all of society) will resume a normal, more naturally sound life. Trust me. … This is a fail-safe plan.

What I hope you come away with after reading this chapter is that playing video games in every form is an antisocial activity with a highly addictive force that can eat up countless hours of your life, especially if you are like me, highly OCD and extremely competitive when it comes to games.

THIRTY THREE

Online Poker

Do you honestly believe that my addictive personality ends with television, Facebook, and video games? Think again.

I am a self-proclaimed gambling addict. (Most people who know me, however, would say that I can be overindulgent when placed in a gambling arena, but that's about all. They're probably more correct than me.) For people like me, gambling used to be an occasional means of escape from an unadventurous, sober life; if you didn't live near Vegas, Atlantic City, a Native American reservation, on the Mississippi, or know a bookie, gambling wasn't easily accessible. You used to have to be motivated to find a way to throw away your money, and you used to have the opportunity to look the person(s) in the eyes that you were donating your money to, especially for a (want-to-be) poker player like me.

Not anymore! Over the past decade the world of gambling evolved from sitting around a table in a smoke-filled casino to sitting at the computer in the home office. While health care officials are ecstatic about the correlated decline of secondhand smoke-related deaths in this country, there is serious concern about the bank accounts of the same people. Especially since 2003, the world of online gambling, most specifically online poker, has boomed. You may ask, "What caused this spark in 2003?" Two words, six syllables, one awesome name … Chris Moneymaker.

In 2003, the aptly named Chris Moneymaker took the poker world by storm by winning the main event at the World Series of Poker in unbelievable fashion. You may ask, "What was so unbelievable about his win?" (You ask a lot of questions!) It was unbelievable because he was the first poker player to win the main event having qualified for it via an online poker site. He won a satellite tournament on PokerStars.com with a $40 buy-in, which gave him entry to the main event where he eventually went on to win $2.5 million. Beyond creating a world of wealth for himself, Moneymaker opened a door to a world for dreamers that did not have the $10,000 lying around for the typical entry fee into the main event; he gave them hope that they could climb to the top of the poker world with a meager start on an online site. What ensued was hysteria.

After Moneymaker's win, TV ratings for poker soared and ESPN reaped the benefits from continuous poker air time. From 2004 to 2010, the online poker world exploded from a $1 billion per year industry to nearly $7 billion per year. (In case you aren't good at math, that translates into a shit-load of online poker). And yours truly was a contributor to both.

You may ask, "What's your big gripe with online poker?" "Do you have a gripe with online poker?" or "When the hell are you going to get to your point in this chapter?" (Again, what's with all of the questions?) In response to your questions, I will make two points:

1. There is something less fun and engaging about playing poker against someone online. Essentially, you sit in a chat room with five to nine other players with whom you never speak; it's nearly impossible to bluff; you can't ever look another player in the eyes and either try to intimidate them or read their

face; the money feels like play money; there are so many more amateurs drawn in that don't know how to play the game (for those poker players reading this book, you know what I mean by this; it is the absolute worst when those knuckleheads stay in a hand they shouldn't and draw luck from the poker gods on the river); and you can't choke in secondhand smoke. It sucks! It absolutely sucks! Not that I'm an intimidating guy, but when I play poker, I want to stare you down (behind my glasses). I want to sense something between fear and confusion in your brain. I want to make you cry on the inside. And I want to get to know you a little bit because I'm just a regular people-person. Online ... well, it's just not the same.

2. I always lose when playing online.

Thankfully, in 2006, former U.S. Senator Bill Frist from the great state of Tennessee appealed to the pain I felt from online poker. He knew that there were people like me out there that feel a sense of sorrow toward the imminent *Death of Human Interaction.* So, Senator Frist (or as I like to refer to him, *Hero*) created legislation that would buck that trend (at least in terms of online gambling in the United States) and set all of us free. (It had *nothing* to do with his conservative agenda and his fight to preserve family values.)

But Senator Frist knew he had to be *creative* when it came to getting this legislation enacted into law, for the Internet machine that the Clinton administration created (led by the father of the Internet, former Vice President Al Gore) had grown too powerful. So, just before Congress adjourned for the 2006 elections, Frist made a "midnight drop" of clauses called the "Unlawful Internet Gambling Enforcement (UIGEA) Act" into the larger, unrelated "Security and Accountability for Every Port (SAFE) Act" knowing that the SAFE Act was a must-pass bill designed to safeguard ports from terrorist infiltration. The UIGEA "prohibits gambling businesses from knowingly accepting payments in connection with the participation of another person in a bet or wager that involves the use of the Internet and that is unlawful under any federal or state law."

Even though, according to a *Wall Street Journal* poll, 85 percent oppose government prohibition of online gambling, I understand the *real* reason why you did what you did, Bill. In my *honest* opinion, 85 percent of the people polled don't get that the *Death of Human Interaction* is upon us. How could they? They're too busy playing *Angry Birds* (now that online gambling is essentially illegal).

The things that I loved (past tense because of Frist's *heroics*) about online poker were that even though the odds were ALWAYS stacked against you, you still always had a shot (even if you suck at poker) and it was easily accessible. The things that I hated about online poker were that you were playing online virtually against other people and that it was easily accessible.

I hated playing online because I love sitting at a table of 9-10 people, seeing that I have great hand, disguising my emotions, and making movements and bets in such a way that might draw in some sucker before I flop over a full house. I love staring someone down in a confident manner as if to tell them "I've got you beat," even though I was bluffing through my teeth (as I often was). I also loved reading the other players' poker faces. Plus the banter at the table was ALWAYS a blast. You haven't seen so many unique (certifiably insane) people all at one table until you've played poker at one of the tables at the Hollywood Park Casino in LA.

When you play poker online, you get none of that! Instead of staring down a 60-year-old dude with a cowboy hat, moustache, and 14 teeth, you casually pay attention to your computer and the move that "ClevelandBronGone" just made. And, as you quickly calculate some odds in your head before you make your next move, you realize that five of the seven other players in the online poker room are using

THE DEATH OF HUMAN INTERACTION

a tool they either purchased or created themselves in order to help them boost their odds.

I often wonder how many ridiculously smart MIT graduates I've played against online that have kicked my ass and how much different it would have been if I faced them in person. Do those nerds actually even know how to play against someone they have to look in the eyes, someone that can't physically intimidate them? Probably not, but again, they are RIDICULOUSLY smart and likely (definitely) realize they have no reason to play the game in person since they constantly kick people's asses like mine with absolute ease online (and make tons of money doing it).

Truth be told, I didn't stop playing poker online because of its antisocial reality. I stopped playing poker online because I was losing; I wasn't losing a ton, but I was losing money I didn't have (often the case when you are at the bottom of the totem pole while working in the movie business). I am writing this book to make LOTS OF MONEY in case online poker becomes legal again so that I can get back into my old habits, feeding my gambling addiction. Thank you for your contribution!

THIRTY FOUR

The End Is Near (Or The Beginning If You Want To Be Fat, Lazy, And Stupid)

There comes a time in every person's life when they are served with a wake-up call. This chapter is yours (as if the entire book isn't).

The moment is finally here where everything has finally come together. For the longest time, people talked about and dreamt about merging two of the world's greatest innovations (time wasters) and putting them into one place so that you no longer have to physically move from one room to the other—or even move your line of sight from one screen to another. The future is upon us! Now, with the Google TV, your computer and your television are one entity. Isn't it grand?

At one point in time, Dell talked about merging the two, but they were never able to get their shit together. Before that, Microsoft's Bill Gates philosophized for years about how one day Microsoft Windows would find its way into people's living rooms and that the television would double as your home computer. He got close with the Xbox; he got damn close. (However, the Xbox has its limitations. It is a separate device whose primary purpose is a video game system and secondary purpose is a computer for your television set.) Google TV doesn't have that limitation. It is LIMITLESS! I mean, isn't it simply grand?

My first and only introduction to Google TV came recently when I visited a friend who had just installed it. I stopped over to have a beer and watch a basketball game with my friends (or at least that was the plan), and they decided to show me their new toy that they got for Christmas.

During the first commercial break, my friend pulled out their keyboard and started scrolling through the applications on the Google TV. There must have been hundreds. He showed me that he can watch YouTube through his television with a mix tape of Blake Griffin's best dunks (instead of just watching some of his new ones in the game we had just been watching). He showed me that he could watch Netflix movies. (I came over to watch a BASKETBALL GAME!) He showed me that he could look up recipes, play games (like *Angry Birds*, of course), look up sports scores (perhaps of the game that I came over to WATCH!), and browse through television channels. (Doesn't the cable box have the capability to perform Google searches, etc.?)

Essentially, with Google TV, he is no longer limited to using his television set for only traditional television capabilities; he can now use his television for that plus everything the Internet has to offer. So, I'll ask it again: Isn't it just grand? Isn't it just grand that there is now such an overwhelmingly powerful device that it can strip the mere mortal of reason (or enough brain power) to walk away from their television set? (If you still have the ability to answer that question, you probably do not yet own a Google TV.)

My answer is "NO! IT IS NOT GRAND! IT IS NOT GRAND AT ALL!" (DO THE CAPS HELP ME MAKE MY POINT? PLEASE WRITE ME A LETTER WHEN YOU TAKE A BREAK FROM USING YOUR GOOGLE TV TO GIVE ME SOME FEEDBACK ON THE CAPS … WHICH WILL NEVER HAPPEN BECAUSE YOU ARE IN A MIND-NUMBING, BRAIN-DUMBING TRANCE.) The two devices that are at the pinnacle of the electronic/Internet/mobile-based technological revolution are the smart phone and Google TV. Those two items alone combine every single thing in your life (as life is understood today) into one device or the other. The only place that technology can go from here is to combine it all—to either put everything from your television into your phone or vice versa. This would mean that you'd be on the go more frequently but ALWAYS dialed into your technology (which wouldn't be a far cry from where most people are today) or you'd always be at home absolutely secluded from the rest of the world. (Isn't that what all the Tech Geeks from Gates to the Friendsters folks to the Match.com folks have always wanted?)

My question is, in the latter scenario (which is seemingly impossible, but not much less surprising if you consider trends from the past couple decades), what does human civilization look like in 20 years? 50 years? 100 years? There have been popular movies made that incorporate the notion of what that future looks like, and it is sad, depressingly sad. Probably the gloomiest movie of all and the one that feels the most spot on to me is *Wall-E*. (Well, not in every capacity—I don't actually believe there is going to be one robot left on Earth whose sole purpose is to clean the entire planet and whose only friend is a cockroach. I don't think there will be another robot that will fly down to Earth that Wall-E will fall in love with at first sight, and who will try to kill Wall-E. That just feels like science fiction. However, the part about the fat people who don't even get out of their chairs anymore as they are completely dialed into their televisions and phones and everything else and eat incredibly fatty foods because they don't know any better ... that all feels very, very true!) Congratulations, Google! You did an excellent job of putting us one step closer toward fulfilling that prophecy!

If you haven't used Google TV before, use it once, but walk away before you get sucked in. If you have never watched Wall-E, *watch it. Once you've done so, reread this chapter and try to tell me that I'm not right. Good luck with that!*

THIRTY FIVE

GPS Has Killed The Wandering Man

I should note, in this chapter, more so than most, I lie to you a number of times. Some lies are big, some lies are small. I trust you to figure out whether I'm lying or not. If you can't, I don't think it matters all that much.

When San Francisco was new to me, I walked its streets one day and got lost. I looked toward the stars to guide me to the baseball stadium only to realize that it was still daytime and the sun was shining brightly. (Plan foiled!) I was still lost.

"Oh no!" I thought to myself. "Whatever will I do? I am just a simple man who does not have the superior navigational skills of your average (or less-than-average) man (an intentionally sexist joke for anyone wondering) and I own no smart phone." (Yes, work provided me with a Blackberry, but I never [hardly] use it outside work.) If I had only listened to my mother, my brother, my wife, my best friend, my other best friend, my roommate, my boss, my coworkers, my aunts and uncles, the random homeless guy I met earlier on the street who walked by me using a smart phone, Steve Jobs, my acquaintances, my other roommate, my neighbors in the projects across the streets, the old people at the retirement community where I volunteer (I don't actually volunteer at a retirement community. I simply wanted to get you to like me), and everyone else in the world who told me to get rid of my "ancient" flip phone and step into a new world (or if I had my work Blackberry with me), I would not be lost right now. If I had only listened, I would have a smart phone with a marvelous GPS system to save the day and tell me how to get to the safe haven called home. But, then again, I'm an idiot! Or am I?

Here's my first thought for all of you people that mock me when you see my flip phone and laugh about its lack of GPS capabilities, those oh-so-wonderful GPS capabilities that guide you around an unfamiliar city like San Francisco. The city is seven miles by seven miles, and it has a 7-Eleven, a taqueria, a gas station, a Starbucks, or a pizza restaurant on every other corner. If worse comes to worst, you won't starve and die. (However, you might have wicked gas or cramps depending on what taqueria you brave.) Secondly, you can walk the city in two hours. Even if you started heading in the absolute wrong direction four times, you would still have plenty of sunlight to find your way home. And, if it is getting dark, you can find a cab, bus, or ask for directions. (But wait ... asking someone for directions would require you to stop and actually speak to someone. That goes against our times, doesn't it?)

The thing is, my rational for not wanting to rely on a GPS has nothing to do with whether or not I find them to be useful; they do provide a very valuable service, one that you might argue to be more useful than most features on a smart phone. I don't want to rely on a GPS because I like getting lost. I don't want to rely on a GPS because I like finding my own way and enjoy the sensation that comes with the unexpected. If you take a moment to think back on some of the most interesting experiences in your life, you might realize that you feel the same. As the famous Steven Tyler said in an Aerosmith song (I think that song was "Amazing"), "Life's a journey, not a destination," or at least it used to be.

This world (all people, places, and things inclusive) is filled with amazement and wonder; it is filled with experiences waiting to stretch your mind and imagination. It is filled with excitement that will make your blood rush and ease your soul. The problem is the shift in human nature. At some point, as our society evolved into one of constant busyness, people became ultimate planners and began siloing their lives as much as possible. People don't want to waste any time because they don't have any to waste; every moment of life must be efficient. Instead of allowing themselves to spend five extra minutes here or there, people decided they must get to their next destination in a timely fashion; there was no room for lingering.

As technology progressed and GPS was developed, people realized they could be even more efficient than ever before. They no longer had to worry about getting lost and losing time. Well, once upon a time, families used to rely on maps and got lost together during a family vacation to Grandma's. They fought and fought and fought about who was to blame—parent vs. parent, parent vs. kid(s), kid vs. kid—it didn't matter. But at the end of it, they pulled off the road to ask for directions at a little diner in a tiny little town in eastern Colorado that served the best rhubarb pie any of them had ever tasted. Now, every time they drive to Grandma's house, they stop in at that little diner with the famous rhubarb pie.

If GPS existed during the time of the family vacation to Grandma's, they never would have stopped into the tiny little town in eastern Colorado, they never would have set foot in that diner, and they never would have tasted that delicious, mouth-watering rhubarb pie. Once upon a time, a man would have accidentally walked into the wrong building in the Lower East Side of Manhattan, bumped into a girl, instantly fell in love, and saw the next 50 years of his life. Once upon a time, an Italian explorer would have set sail for East India only to discover a new world.

On that particular day when I got lost in San Francisco, I had one of those experiences, one of those once-in-a-lifetime experiences that only happens when you least expect it, and it never would have happened if I had a GPS on me that day.

On that particular day, as I was wandering the streets trying to find my way to AT&T Park to see the Giants play my New York Mets, I realized I was running incredibly late and decided to ask for help with directions. (After all, the Giants were playing THE New York Mets, the team I have idolized my entire life, and the stars weren't out yet.) The first couple people just completely ignored me. When I approached them, they were on their smart phones; when they walked away from me, they were still on their smart phones (jackasses!).

I thought about my approach. "Why is this so hard? Am I doing something wrong? Do I look sketchy? What's that smell? Oh, God! What's that smell? Oh, it's just the homeless person rubbing up against me." I realized that all the people I approached were clearly under the age of 40. These should have been my peeps, but they weren't. These people lived in a tech-central, antisocial world. I realized what I have known all along: I am an old soul living in a 29-year-old's body. I understand a 70-year-old way better than a 21-year-old, a 27-year-old, or a 35-year-old. Moments after coming to this conclusion, I saw an elderly black man wearing a Giants hat; he appeared kind but, more importantly, did not have a smart phone in his hands. So, I approached him:

Me: "Hello."
Elderly Black Man: "Hello, to you, my boy."
Me: "Nice day today."
Elderly Black Man: "Oh yes, my boy. It's one of the finest this city has seen in years!"
Me: "Really? I didn't know that. I actually just moved to the city only a few weeks ago."
Elderly Black Man: "My boy, you have done yourself a service. This is a marvelous city. Say hey, where are you from?"
Me: "Well, I was born in Pennsylvania, went to overnight summer camps in the Poconos when I was younger, went to college in upstate New York even though I considered going to LA for college—"

THE DEATH OF HUMAN INTERACTION

Elderly Black Man: "My boy, I am sorry to interrupt, but I am old with only so much time left on this planet. ... I meant, where did you just move from?"

Me: "Oh ... I just moved here from Seattle."

Elderly Black Man: "Say hey, my boy. That is a wonderful city."

Me: "Yes. It was pretty good. I mean, most of the women are ugly, it rains a lot, grunge music died a decade ago, but at least it's got some great outdoors."

Elderly Black Man: "Grunge what?"

Me: "You know ... Nirvana!"

Elderly Black Man: "Nirvana? Isn't that the state of being free from suffering?"

Me: "In Sramanic thought, yes. In Hindi philosophy, it is the union with the Supreme Being through mosksha. But, in this case, I meant Nirvana the band. You know, like Kurt Cobain? The guy that went click and bang with a shotgun to his right-side temple awhile back."

Elderly Black Man: "My boy, I am afraid I am not familiar with him, but that sounds like a sad story. Say hey, you're from Pennsylvania and you're wearing a New York Mets hat?"

Me: "Of course I am! I am the biggest Mets fan there is! I could name the opening day starting lineup every year for the Mets since their start!"

Elderly Black Man: "Say hey, can you tell me what old crafty veteran split time between first base and the outfield in the 1972 and 1973 seasons?"

Me: "That's easy ... Willie Mays!"

Elderly Black Man: "Willie Mays is right! Say hey, it's nice to meet you, my boy!"

Me: "You are Willie Mays?" [He nodded his head to acknowledge.] "Oh my gosh! You ARE Willie Mays! This is ... this is ... this is ... uh ... umm ... uh ... umm ... this is INCREDIBLE!"

Elderly Black Man: "Say hey, my boy ... Given that you're a Mets fan, you don't happen to be going to the game, do you?"

Me: "Actually, well yeah. At least I am trying to. You see, like I said, I am new to the city and the stars aren't out yet, so my usual navigational tools are useless. I can hardly tell which direction is north around here."

Elderly Black Man: "Say hey ... you seem like a nice young man. I happen to be going to the game. I can show you the way if you'd like? Perhaps I'll even get you a ticket to the owners' box so we can finish this conversation there, but you might have to hide your hat if it's a bad night for the Giants. Say hey ... what do you think?"

Me: "Did the 'Say Hey Kid' really just invite me to the baseball game with him? Mr. Mays, I'd be a fool to say no."

Elderly Black Man: "Please, call me Willie."

Though this Willie Mays story is clearly a lie, there is a moral to the story, which is a truth; that is if you're always focused on the destination, you'll never get to enjoy the journey; meaning, if you streamline your life (or in this instance, the trip to the ballpark), you will miss out on the random occurrences that make the world worthwhile.

While my story is fake, there have been countless times in my life where I went in the wrong direction because I didn't know any better, didn't have technology to save the day, and ended up finding a beautiful beach, a fantastic restaurant, a funny story, and in some cases, a new friend. If you try living life without a GPS, you might discover the same.

Now, you may ask yourself why I would make up such a ridiculous story. It was to make a point, but beyond that, who really knows? Perhaps for entertainment value?

THIRTY SIX

Wikipedia To The Rescue

Wikipedia, I love you.

Throughout this entire book, I have been mildly to incredibly hard on most forms of technology and associated services developed within the past hundred years with a sharp focus on more recent decades. (After reading through most of this book, I hope you can relate to or at least understand my opinions. If not, too bad. You already paid for the book and my publisher has it baked into the deal with all distribution outlets that there is a strict "no refund" policy on the greatest book about the *Death of Human Interaction* that I have ever written.) Despite the messages ingrained in each chapter, I am not a completely cynical bastard. I do believe that every so often a company (even an interwebs-based one) creates something so fantastic that we cannot overlook its perfection. My friends, that outstanding accomplishment of which I speak is none other than Wikipedia. Honestly, is there any mobile or computer-based website in the world that provides more benefits to our lives than Wikipedia? (For those of you that say Google does, you are probably correct, but why don't you just shut up? This is my book!) Let me try to explain why I feel this way.

When I was growing up in the '80s and '90s, if I ever had a question that I did not know the answer to (which every young'n has), if I ever needed to find a source for a research assignment (Stupid school! Why'd you make me get my learn on?), or if I ever wanted to prove someone wrong (which I loved to do and was able to do because I got my learn on. Thank you, school!), I had to put real effort into getting the info. A sound place to start was by asking my parents, but, like all mere mortals, their knowledge base was limited (although they would probably argue that point with you). I also had the opportunity to ask my friends, their parents, my teachers, the mailman, my little league coach, and the local butcher amongst others, but they all knew only so much. I could not rely solely on the people in my life to provide me with what I sought; so I had to dive into books, journals, magazines, and newspapers. This meant a trip to the library to start shredding through resources.

The first challenge going to the library was learning the Dewey Decimal System (something kids today are likely unfamiliar with) in order to find the right books, journals, magazines, and newspapers. Oftentimes when I identified a resource that might bring me the right answers, someone else already had it checked out. For example, it was not unusual for me to find my way over to the encyclopedia section in an attempt to find my answers. Once there, I would discover that the volumes I needed (let's say "R") from each of the 1983-1992 editions were currently being used by other people, which meant I had to settle on the 1982 edition. This became problematic if I needed information about some turmoil on the Rhone River from 1984. (This is not a history lesson. Don't look up turmoil on the Rhone River in 1984 because you probably won't find anything there. It is what I call a bullshit example I came up with to better make my point. However, if you insist, look it up.) The point being, during my formative years, getting the information I needed was often a slow, tedious process that sometimes led me to a place somewhere between diminishing hope and shit-out-of-luck.

Today and since the birth of Wikipedia in January 2001 (I know this because I just used Wikipedia to look up information about the

THE DEATH OF HUMAN INTERACTION

history of Wikipedia), times they've been a changin'. In January 2001, Jimmy Wales and Larry Sanger launched not just a website but a way of life that has made my existence and probably everyone else's so much easier. The ingenious name—a combination of the Hawaiian word "wiki," meaning "quick," and the "-pedia" portion of the word "encyclopedia"—is only a tiny reason why I love this site (very clever, Jimbo and Lar).

The reason I love this site so much is that it rids my life of the tediousness described in the previous paragraph, especially in situations where I want to prove people wrong. (It's possible that I may get a little competitive from time to time.) If I need information at the touch of a button that is mostly reliable (or so I'm convinced), all I have to do is Wikipedia it! The only real barriers I have between me and timely Wikipedia-style fact checking or discovery at any given time is a wireless connection and enough computer battery life remaining. (I'd suggest that a smart phone makes it slightly easier because I wouldn't have to have my laptop on me at all times; however, by now all of you know that I want to be the very last dumb phone user in existence, so the point is null. Every single teenager living in the most impoverished countries in the world will have smart phones before I come around. That's not a thought; it's a promise. UPDATE: As you read at the beginning of this book, my flip phone finally died, forcing me to get a smart phone. This happened after I wrote this chapter and proves me wrong—I will not be the last living sole on the planet without a smart phone.)

Three particular instances during which I especially love to use Wikipedia include:

1. When I am curious, which is all the damn time! An example, perhaps, could be if I were to read a magazine article on my way to work about the world's greatest sushi chef, who happens to live in Omaha, Nebraska (something that clearly would make sense considering all the salmon, tuna, yellowtail, and

eel that fill the bodies of water near Nebraska). If it caught my interest to learn more (which it clearly would because I love eating sushi, making sushi, and Omaha, Nebraska), I would immediately look to learn more about his background using Wikipedia the moment I got into the office. (Again, if I had only come around to smart phone technology, I would have gotten that information even sooner. However, if I had a smart phone, I probably would have been playing *Angry Birds* rather than reading the article about this insanely awesome sushi chef. UPDATE: This is often the case!)

2. When I am playing bar trivia. The way I see it, there are two ways to guarantee yourself a victory at bar trivia: (1) Find a friend that has absorbed way too much useful information throughout the years and always bring him/her along. (My friend that falls into that category unfortunately moved far, far away from me to the wild metropolis of Kansas City to start a family ... greedy bastard! Greg, I miss you, my bar trivia captain! Come home to me!) (2) Use your smart phone to look up all the right answers on Wikipedia while you play. (This works almost as well as having Greg by my side.) Obviously this is considered cheating, so try to be slick (which shouldn't faze you much if you've already gone down the path of cheating online, much like me [refer to chapter 22]). You should probably hold your smart phone under the table, behind a menu, or even step away to the bathroom in order to pull this off without being caught. In my situation, I'd have to borrow someone else's smart phone. (UPDATE: No more!)

3. When I am writing this book. Since I am looking for only an iota of fact for most of the stories I tell, I don't want to stress myself with too much research. (I am a much lazier person than people give me credit for.) Wikipedia has been my best friend throughout this book. Whenever I can't quite remember the history of something, or I need a quick bio or some other

THE DEATH OF HUMAN INTERACTION

miscellaneous information, I open up Wikipedia and BAM; within a couple minutes, I have all the information I need. The only complication to this is that after I find the information I need, I am dialed into the article, which leads me to read through additional information that is of absolutely no use to me at that or probably any given time. Then that information triggers another thought in my brain, which leads me down the path of about five more Wikipedia searches. About 45 minutes later, I snap out of my trance, not remembering why I originally started searching through Wikipedia in the first place. Every so often I find my way to where I was trying to go before I started searching Wikipedia.

In addition to everything else, I also love this website because it is a nonprofit organization with a commendable social purpose. Even though the factualness of the website is often questioned (by the evil *Encyclopedia Britannica* media empire ... the bastards that always used to show up at your front door trying to sell you an encyclopedia set only minutes after the Cutco kids tried to sell you knives and the Jehovah's Witnesses tried to convince you to join their cult), Wikipedia has shown time and time again that it has a pretty solid rate of accuracy. This means that Wikipedia provides pretty reliable information (including loads of educations informational) to people all over the world free of charge (assuming they can find their way onto a computer with an Internet connection, which is becoming very common almost everywhere these days). This is one of the truly great things about the Internet—its ability to easily provide valuable, educational information at the speed of thought.

I may have overstated its perfectionness earlier in this chapter, but Wikipedia, for the most part, is a website that displays benefits of the Internet.

THIRTY SEVEN

Technology Isn't All Bad

Despite my many criticisms through the first 30+ chapters of everything from radio to television to cell phones to social media to video games and beyond, I must admit that technology isn't all bad. (Please refer back to chapter 38 as one example of this.)

I would be a complete liar (like Jim Carrey in the movie *Liar Liar*) if I said with conviction that technology is ALL bad. I do not believe that in the least. Technology and our continued investment and advancement in various forms of it are actually, in general, good things. My displeasure corresponds more directly with the overwhelming abuse of technology by individuals and the amount of time wasted by so many smart, innovative thinkers who spend the better parts of their lives thinking of ways to increase user usage of such ridiculous products as virtual social networking, among other things. (As I've clearly made my point time and time again throughout this book, if you want to go do something, go do it. If you want to strike up a conversation with someone, strike up a conversation with someone. Don't waste your time and your life futzing around with technologies that are designed to be substitutes for what any human being has the capability to do—communicate!)

Think about what science and technology have given us over the past 100-150 years. We have witnessed the invention of the light bulb, the airplane, the automobile, the telephone, the radio, the television, the computer, and the Internet. The world can function at what would have been unthinkable speeds in Lincoln's time. And, with all the advancements in these technologies have come advancements in medical science, electrical science, education, mechanical science, etc.

Using all sorts of devices that are beyond my personal understanding, we as a world have been able to come up with cures and vaccinations for certain types of diseases that once appeared unstoppable, and we can deliver them around the globe in a timely fashion. We are better at developing pharmaceuticals and educating the public in ways to sustain healthier and longer lives. We can even utilize electronics to act as tools in performing critical surgeries that can save people's lives.

For example, while I was in graduate school at the University of Washington, I attended a lecture by Bill Gates that was part of his retirement (from Microsoft) tour. During this lecture, Gates spoke about the role that Microsoft has played in changing the medical landscape. He told us a hypothetical story of how a surgeon living in Sweden, the world's outright expert in a unique specialty, now had the opportunity to use video conferencing technology to walk a surgeon living in India through a complicated procedure in real time. My initial thought to this was, "This is truly remarkable!" Sadly, my second thought was, "How long until people abuse this technology?" (Not long, it turns out. Has anyone heard of Skype [please refer to chapter 16], which now happens to be owned by Microsoft?)

Technology can also have an enormous impact on the world from an environmental standpoint. As an electric utility employee for more than the last four years, I can tell you that the future of the energy business is absolutely amazing. At some point in time, we will have the opportunity to intelligently utilize our energy generation and offtake to a point of absolute precision mostly because of smarter technologies that can better speak to one another. It is and will be incredible to watch devices in our homes and in our offices interact in an intelligent fashion. (I'm not implying that people should buy more guns to protect themselves against their microwave; their microwave isn't going to grow legs and try to attack them. If you believe that it will one day attack you, you probably deserve it.) What this means is that your household appliances will be able to communicate with one another in code that will tell your dishwasher to run on less power during a certain time of day or when another appliance, like your dryer, needs to take on more energy usage. Your appliances will provide your homes with better energy usage, meaning less consumption. These technologies will also better inform the grid (the utility) with better data, which should hopefully lead to less power generation or, in some cases, more power generation coming from clean, renewable energies like wind and solar power. Again, our energy future is absolutely amazing mostly because of advanced technologies which are (or will be) enabled by the Internet and mobile technologies.

On top of this, there are also companies out there that are working on building upon our technological advancements to educate farmers. In the developed world, this comes in the form of better information provided both by the Internet and mobile resources regarding weather patterns, amongst other things. In developing countries, farmers would more readily gain access to the best agricultural practices to both increase production and decrease water usage.

Education in general is another big area where technology plays a huge role. For example, there are mobile app developers working on bridging the gap in math and language education all over the developing world. Organizations such as the Gates Foundation are working around the clock to figure out new ways to provide opportunities to the seemingly forgotten low-income, underserved people—both domestic and international. There is a huge gap between the rich and the poor in this world in terms of education; technology can serve as a means for bridging that gap.

My problem with Bill's lecture is not that I don't believe in the wonderful benefits of technology; my problem is that he completely dismisses the notion of human nature. Yes, video conferencing technology provides an enormous benefit to the world 0.001 percent of the time. It functions only as another distraction in our lives 73 percent of the time. (The other 26.999 percent of the time it's just kind of irrelevant.) Yes, technology produces a major impact in terms of the environment, education, agriculture, and about three dozen other areas, but more often than not, people don't care about the relevant uses; they care more about the irrelevant uses! They care more about the irrelevant uses because they are entertaining, fun, and easy. They care about them because there is more time in the day than most of us realize, and we *need* something to fill the void. People are afraid of living on an island. They care more about the irrelevant uses because they are popular and they don't want to be left behind.

I give kudos to Bill Gates and to other technological geniuses we have encountered throughout the years for their realization that even though they want to make a dollar, there are opportunities for good to come of all their hard work. They don't have to care, but they do (and so should we). The challenge is overcoming human nature.

THIRTY EIGHT

A Whole New Antisocial World

I highlighted some of the good. Now let's get back to the bad.

I want to go back to the days when people were social. I may sound about 50 years older than I am. (It's possible that 80-year-olds are the only ones who understand my perspective. It's also possible that they will be the only ones to read this book considering they are the only people who still possess the functional ability to read as their brains haven't dissolved into dust due to the popular mobile game *Angry Birds*.) But I remember a time when people put themselves out there in public places and generally got very communicative responses from their fellow man or woman. Bars, buses, banks, coffee shops, sporting events, parties, etc.—in any one of those settings, someone could strike up a solid conversation with an absolute stranger if they so desired.

Today, well, today, the world is a very different place; you can do all your banking either via your home computer or at an ATM; you can order food, coffee, or anything else and have it delivered; AND you no longer have to go to sporting events because the viewing experience watching it on your 75-inch high-definition flat screen television is just as good as being there. Because of the luxuries in their lives, people no longer want in-person, face-to-face interaction (or so they've convinced themselves). People simply want to move on their way as quickly and as undisturbed as possible.

People walk through life in a bubble. (No, you silly fool, not an actual bubble. Who actually owns a bubble anyway?) Bubbles such as those created by iPods, smart phones, iPads, portable televisions, whatever, are seemingly impenetrable. (To the sci-fi fans that read this book—again the 80-year-old sci-fi fans—it's like a force field.)

I'll give you an example. Right now I happen to be sitting next to a guy (let's call him "Ging" because he happens to be an absolute *ginger*—red hair, very pale skin, and lots of freckles for those of you who don't know what a *ginger* is) on a four-hour flight from San Francisco to Chicago. Since I have been seated next to him, Ging hasn't said one word to me; as far as I can tell, he hasn't even acknowledged my existence. (I have tested this theory by releasing one fart after another in his direction, the result of the spicy turkey chili I just ate. He hasn't even winced, which is surprising given that I'm pretty sure I knocked out the guy next to him. Perhaps I overshot?) Instead, he has been passionately watching DirecTV (right now he is dialed into Tosh.O, which, if you haven't seen it, is a show entirely focused on the same stupid YouTube clips I refer to in chapter 27) with intermittent breaks to play with his iPad during the commercials. He doesn't even have a clue that I have been writing about him for the past 25 minutes. (I'm a slow typer—and thinker. Lay off me!) He hasn't looked over once. I will now experiment by physically turning my computer to meet Ging's face as if to invite him to read everything that I write. (If you can picture this situation, I now have my computer screen angled away from me. I type one key at a time and lean my head to the side to better see what I am typing.)

I type: The red-headed ginger sitting to my right looks like a life-size Raggedy Andy.

His response: (Nothing!)

THE DEATH OF HUMAN INTERACTION

I type: I've seen road kill with more personality than Ging.

His response: (Not even a curious expression as to why I have my computer facing him and why I keep looking at him after every key stroke.)

I decide to turn the computer back to face me.

I could write anything about him right now and he would not have a clue. It is absolutely incredible. He is so zoned in on his technologies and completely unaware of his surroundings. If one of the two people sitting to either side of him were to be set on fire, he wouldn't have a clue. (In this scenario, I hope it'd be the dude I knocked out with my farts. I don't want to be set on fire. I just really, really don't.)

If I were in his place and someone was so non-discreetly writing a chapter about me in a book discussing the topic of the death of human interaction and how technology gets in between us in the routine of our lives, I would call that person out. I would make them feel shamed and uncomfortable for the remainder of the flight like an ideal Jewish mother would do to her son in almost any situation (while turning my butt ever so slightly in their direction and casually passing gas for the remainder of the plane ride). Well, I suppose Panzer wins this round. Or does technology win?

The reality is that Ging and his actions are not completely unnatural, at least not anymore. I confidently assume that given the devices that presently exist, the vast majority of people in the United States today are more prone to be dialed in to technology than not. Honestly, the only people that seem to want to communicate in a public place anymore are the people that are either too old to understand the new-age technologies or too broke to afford them (or too chicken-shit to try to steal them ... WUSSIES! I'd use another word that rhymes with this but it would really piss off my wife. Yes, I am whipped.). People who fall into those categories are 96.5 percent more likely to strike up or maintain a dialogue with others in a public setting than anyone outside those categories. I know this for a fact based on an informal, NON-scientific, highly unstructured study I have been performing over the past eight months since I have been living in San Francisco and riding public transportation on a regular basis. (I should also mention that I do not know the ages or incomes of my subjects, but that point is primarily irrelevant.)

Positive Resistance

Since I started writing this chapter, I spent some time in Chicago (which should be obvious to anyone reading THIS chapter as I mentioned toward the beginning of it that I sat next to Ging on a flight from SF to Chicago). During my time in Chicago, I rode the L Train several times.

The one thing I found to be warming about the L Train on a cold winter's day in Chicago was this: When the doors shut and the train starts moving, a recorded message almost immediately comes on the loud speaker saying something along the lines of "Please be mindful of others when using your cell phones or when listening to audio devices." I do wish the message was a bit bolder, saying something along the lines of "Turn all your motherf*@king electronic devices the f*@k off and put them the f*@k away in your f*@king purse, your f*@king pocket, or your f*@king bag; no one is going to f*@king call you, your f*@king text messages are a f*@king waste of time, and you f*@king suck at mobile video games. Now assh@le, turn to your right and introduce yourself to the dipsh%t (interesting person) sitting next to you. Ask them about their day; learn about someone completely new. Who knows, you might have something in common. Or, at the very least, it will likely lead to some good f*@king stranger-sex tonight. Remember to please fasten your condom when inserted into unfamiliar crevices." The current message, in my opinion, is a start in the right direction. It ultimately suggests that people who decide they want to be antisocial in what could be a social setting should not distract from those who actually want to be social and not the other way around. Thank you, Chicago! Other major cities, did you get the memo? If not, just shoot me an e-mail; I'll be sure to forward it on to you.

Silver Lining

While I would like to suggest having technologies at one's disposal in a public setting is all bad, that is certainly not the case. In fact, I'd be a hypocrite (I am a hypocrite, but I'll dive into more detail regarding this in chapter 40) if I did not admit that there have been times when I too have used technology in what could be social settings. I have even gone as far as using devices as a means to get or keep me out of certain conversations. (Hopefully you won't be too hard on me after reading on.) One example of this came during my first few months in San Francisco.

Having moved to a US city that actually has decent public transportation, I was extremely excited that I no longer had to commute to work alone; I now had 40-50 people sharing the ride with me every morning, people with whom I could chat during my trips to and from work. One of my first days riding my particular bus route to work, my excitement was fulfilled; I struck up a conversation with a guy in his mid-50s while we both stood at the bus stop awaiting our ride. On first account, he seemed quite normal and nice. When we boarded the busy bus, our conversation ended as we were separated by other people.

A few days later, I ran into that guy again. We started another conversation that began at the bus stop, but this time continued onto the bus. Surprisingly, we found ourselves on a fairly open bus and were able to grab two seats. This conversation also started off pretty good. However, looking at it in retrospect, for the sake of our budding commuter friendship, the conversation should have ended at the bus stop before he ever had enough time to tell me more about his profession.

A couple minutes into the conversation, he began explaining to me that he was a lawyer that worked on cases focused on asbestos-related cancer victims. At first, that sounded wonderful, especially considering how he marketed himself to me; at a high level, he made it seem like he was a crusader fighting for the unfortunate cancer victims that had their worlds turned upside down due to the terrible realities of asbestos. Because I'm an inquisitive SOB, I had to ask a few more questions. (Sorry, Mom. It's a figure of speech. I didn't mean to call you a "B.") What I discovered was that I was way off! The turning point in the conversation went something like this:

Guy: My job is truly so rewarding.
Me: I bet it is. I mean, it's wonderful that you're fighting the good fight. They truly need your help.
Guy: It's true! For so long, they have been unfairly subjected to such negative publicity that has dampened the industry.
Me: The industry?
Guy: Yes. The asbestos industry.
Me: Wait … what?
Guy: The asbestos industry. It's been unfairly subjected to negative publicity for way too long.
Me: Hold up! Are you telling me you work FOR the asbestos industry?
Guy: Uh, yeah.
Me: [WHAT THE F*@K?] I thought you said you work on behalf of the cancer patients affected by the asbestos industry?
Guy: [He laughs hard.] No! I work on behalf of the asbestos industry. Essentially I work on the settlement cases with those cancer patients. I get paid by trying to beat them in a legal setting, by keeping them from getting paid. [He smiles and laughs again.] Work for the cancer patients? Hahaha! No!

At that moment I realized I was face-to-face with one of the worst human beings I have ever met. Honestly, what kind of assh@le is so proud that he deprives cancer patients of both the money they need

THE DEATH OF HUMAN INTERACTION

and the money they deserve? To be frank, I was absolutely sickened by how terrible this man was. I could not wait to get away from him. When I finally did, I hoped I'd never see him again, but I knew that wouldn't be the case as we were on the same bus route and seemed to be on fairly similar schedules.

A few days later he haunted me again with his presence. I was the second-to-last person to board the bus and found the second-to-last seat. As I sat down, the bus started to shut the door, but as it did, a hand flew out and blocked it from shutting. A moment later, Asbestos-guy's face appeared (as if straight out of a horror movie). He immediately scanned the bus for any seats, saw that the last seat on the bus happened to be situated directly next to me, and sat down with a smile.

That day I was visibly sick as a dog (not only because of Asbestos-guy), but Asbestos-guy did not give a rat's ass. Nope, he was excited to tell me more about the horrible things that made him who he was. He started by discussing a traffic violation that he admitted (to me) being at fault for, but how he aggressively fought it because he is better than other people and doesn't deserve to be held to the law like everyone else. Then, he dove into the topic of hit and runs; he first asked me what kind of car I drove. When I was curious as to why he wanted to know, he suggested that he wanted to avoid hitting my car. When he clarified further, he told me that he regularly performed the act of hit and run all over town (and he was proud of it). From that point forward, I had nothing left in the tank to even fake an interest in a conversation with him. He made me cringe all the way down to the core. I decided I could take no more.

The next few times I saw him at the bus stop or on the bus, I made sure to have my cell phone in hand and ready to go. If I saw him walking in my direction, I would immediately call or text someone, anyone. There were many times that didn't faze him, which lead me to outright ignoring him. I began to act as if he wasn't even there. Essentially, I did what I despise ... I used technology to create an invisible barrier around me in order to shut him out. Do I feel bad about it? Not in the least. After all, Asbestos-guy is en evil dick! In that situation, I used the power of technology for good, for self-preservation.

Silver Lining Part Two

A few months ago I went to an allergist to get tested for pretty much every type of allergy imaginable. What I found out is that I probably should live in a bubble as I am allergic to a bunch of things including dust.

While I was there, I happened to meet a nice, seemingly sane older lady as I waited to get the results of my allergy tests. At first, she mentioned that she had some pretty serious allergies that needed attention. I could relate. Then she started complaining about her medical provider, the facility, and the staff. It is not unusual to hear complaints about the various components of our health care system in the U.S., so I continued to listen to her concerns. However, this led her to start babbling about how the medical staff was trying to kill her, which then sent her down a course of questioning the philosophy of medicine altogether. (Not the physicians, not the prescriptions, not the facilities, not the legislation—no, she questioned the philosophy of medicine.)

I began to realize that it was possible I misjudged her when I first assessed her sanity level. It was very likely that this lady lost her mind ages ago, if she ever even had it in the first place. There were now a million questions running through my mind about this crazy woman; the only definitive thing I knew about our conversation moving forward was that I would have to get out of it as quickly as humanly possible. At that moment, I reached into my bag and pulled out my phone.

I started texting people I hadn't in years just to give me a reason to turn away from this woman. That didn't slow her down a bit. She carried on our conversation for the next 25 minutes without any response from me. Looking back on that occasion, I was disappointed with

THE DEATH OF HUMAN INTERACTION

myself that I went against my nature by purposely using technology to get in the way; however, I was even more pissed off that my attempt to use technology in that fashion failed miserably in a time of need! (Do I really feel bad about my attempts to ignore that lady? Not in the least. She was batshit crazy!)

As a follow-up to the airplane story from earlier in the chapter, once the plane landed, Ging IMMEDIATELY unplugged his headphones from the DirecTV, pulled out his iPhone, and started listening to some tunes while playing a game. Does anyone else qualify this as disturbing behavior?

THIRTY NINE

Blog Rant

As we near the end of the book, you may be asking yourself the same question that loads of other people asked me throughout the process of writing this book, "Why don't you just write a blog instead?" Well, on one hand, thank you for the question. On the other, pipe down and read on.

In 1997, the French chemist Philippe Jean Blog designed a tool on the World Wide Web that allowed every single person who aspired to be a writer (but was either crap or had something of sheer irrelevance to discuss that no one outside—and sometimes inclusive of—their immediate group of friends had any interest in reading about) a forum within which to write and distribute. This capability would later be named the "blog."

You might ask yourself, "Why would we want every single person to have the ability to write personal stories or opinions in a forum that is so easy to distribute? (We don't!) Wouldn't that fill the world with an abundant number of painfully dull stories and countless inaccurate portrayals of fact that would reach unsuspecting audiences at the speed of light? (YES!) And wouldn't that lead to a situation of information overload?" (WITHOUT A DOUBT!) You would be right to ask yourself these questions. But the best one to ask yourself is, "The inventor of the 'blog' was a chemist?" *(Please refer back to the first page of this book.)*

Ever since I started writing this book, people have told me that it sounds like a great blog idea. Here is how a typical conversation goes:

Random Friend 1: Where the hell have you been? I haven't seen you in ages. Don't you want to come out and party anymore? Panzer ... Don't be a "Panzee!"

Aaron: First time I've heard that one. Good one, Random Friend 1.

Random Friend 1: Seriously, though, where the hell have you been? You should come hang out.

Aaron: Well, I'm going through a quarter-life crisis realizing that there are things I want to accomplish in my life that don't involve getting hammered every weekend night and then wondering the entire next day why my head feels like it's constantly being jackhammered.

Random Friend 1: So...

Aaron: So, remember how I always said I wanted to write a book?

Random Friend 1: No.

Aaron: That's 'cause you are blacked-out drunk every time I see you.

Random Friend 1: Probably so. I did just have seven to 13 shots of Patron. What are you writing about? [His phone rings, so he says to me ...] Hold on one sec. [To the person on the phone ...] Yeah, we're at McClellands. Come on by. I'm with Panzer. [Pause.] Yeah, he is a "Panzee." [His phone conversation continues in a similar fashion for another four minutes until ...] Alright, I'll see you in a bit. [He hangs up the phone and turns back to me ...] Random Friend 2 is on his way. What were we talking about?

Me: My book.

Random Friend 1: Oh yeah. What's it about?

Me: It's about exactly what you just did.

Random Friend 1: What do you mean?

Me: The book is called *The Death of Human Interaction: A Sociologist's and Psychologist's Perspective from a Non-Expert in Both Areas.*

Random Friend 1: HAAAA! Sounds funny. What's it about?

Me: It's about technology getting in the way of natural human interaction, like with you answering your cell phone a few moments ago. ... In doing so—and proceeding to have a five-minute conversation—you were a rude jackass to me, the person directly in front of you that you were just having a conversation with.

Random Friend 1: Ha! True that! That sounds like a very relevant topic, but wouldn't that be even better written as a blog?

When I ask them what they mean, they feed me some bullshit that they truly buy into, such as, "If you want to rant about something, start a blog," "A blog is a great place to share your ideas and opinions," and "Blogging is the free flow of thoughts expressed at its finest."

The first problem with that rationale is that I am OCD. If you don't know what OCD is, go to Wikipedia.com, type "OCD" into the search bar, and press enter. My OCD causes me to grow frantic and stressed if I do not live within a world of structure. By writing a book, I am forced to develop a framework. There is a start and an end, and it will likely be no longer than 100 pages (at least that was the plan ... what page are we on again?) because my publisher won't be able to afford a longer book for the pennies of revenue this book will generate. Also, let's be honest, because I'm typing this book on a computer with access to the Internet (as all computers over the past 15 years have had), I have the mental capacity of a goldfish. It is guaranteed that I will watch Susan Boyle's "I Dreamed a Dream" 10 times before I finish writing the first draft of this chapter while singing along out loud at the coffee shop where I am currently writing; there is no way I'd be able to retain focus.

Can you imagine the level of disarray I would expose myself to in writing a blog? A blog is endless; it is a chore. It comes with the obligation to write something once or twice a week with each entry being a ridiculous length because THERE IS NO LIMIT TO A BLOG. I would stay up till all hours of the night cleaning my apartment, eating certain types of food, and going through the rest of my OCD rituals before I even got started. Sleep would become second fiddle. I would lose my job because I would either be brain-dead in meetings or always thinking of the next paragraph or entry to write (which I do anyway). My OCD is a curse; a blog would surely be my demise.

Problemo numero dos ... I am clearly writing this book because I believe it will bring me fame and fortune. Once this book reaches the shelves, it will immediately become a *New York Times* best seller. FOX will reach out to me to create a television show and Internet series based on my book and my life (both of which will completely negate some core messages of this book, but I won't mind because it will make me rich). Then, with fortune in hand, I will travel the world and write books based on my experiences that rival those of Bill Bryson. (I'm coming after you, Bill!) If I were to put my thoughts into a blog instead, no one would ever read them with the exception of my mother, who in turn would disown me for using her as an example time and time again. At least when I become rich and famous subsequent to the publication of this book, she'll still claim me as her son, anticipating I'll

THE DEATH OF HUMAN INTERACTION

introduce her to Oprah (when I make it into her book club) and buy her every new piece of consumer technology upon release.

A blog is too large of a business endeavor with no financial return on my blood, sweat, and tears investment. In order to get my family and friends to read it, I will have to deal with conversations such as:

Me: Hey, I wrote a blog. You should check it.

Random Friend 3: No way! I wrote a blog as well. Mine's about my fluffy, adorable little cat, Rosie. I'll read yours if you read mine.

Me: Yeah ... that sounds *great*. "Rosie" ... the cat. *Can't wait. Yay* ...

I could just tell them I will read their blog with no real intentions of doing so, but then that would just make me a liar. So now I'd either be stuck wasting my time reading about the cute, adorable way that this little cat (which I would grow to loathe) knocks her little (equally cute) mouse toy around or have an overbearing guilty conscience. The fine line between sanity and lunacy would be crossed, and I wouldn't even have a dollar in my pocket to show for it.

Alternatively, if I ask them to read my book (for $29.95), no one will be able to make a similar request of me because none will have authored one; none of my time will be wasted reading ridiculous blogs about cats, art, teeth cleaning, bondage, etc. (Actually, I might read the blog about bondage out of curiosity.) It is a failsafe plan. I know this for a fact because I choose my friends in a very selective manner. I choose the drunkest and dumbest people at bars and parties to become my friends. I do this because, comparatively, it makes me look good. I also know that none of them will one day find the attention span between drunken spells to pen a book and subsequently ask me to read it.

If I were to write a blog, in order to go one step further and get a committed following (all my friends and family across the world), I'd fall into an endless pattern of advertising and networking. I'd have to show up at birthdays of "friends" that I haven't spoken with in years (for good reason). I'd have to send those wedding presents I meant to send three years back. I'd have to apologize for getting drunk and hooking up with his sister or her mother or their grandmother. In order to get my readers, I'd have to sacrifice time and lose my dignity over and over again. Is it really worth it in the end?

Problem three is that this is not just a rant of any sort. You might be asking yourself throughout this book, "What the hell is this guy talking about? Is there a point?" There is, and even if you can't identify what it is, that is what makes this book far more than a rant. I am telling the history and consequences of the deterioration of the extroverted man. If I wrote a blog instead, I'd fuel the flame that I'd like to put out in the sense that people who want to read my "rant" would have to find a place with WiFi, open up their computers, log on to the server, open up the Internet, and find my blog using some obscure search engine because Google, Yahoo, and Bing will all have blocked me due to the nature of this book. Then they might read none of it, some of it, or all of it before further poking around the Internet and losing another three hours of their day and their life. A book is simple; you can pick it up and put it down as you please. You can read it on an airplane, on the bus, in a park, or on the go. A book offers you more freedom of mind and body ... and you don't need a battery or outlet to operate it (unless you are using an e-reader—damn you Amazon and Apple). But, beyond all the luxuries of reading a book over a blog, there is an amazing rush that you get when you feel that (hopefully recycled) paper in your hand and you get a sniff of it in the air as your turn from page to page.

I remember when the Disney Afternoon was cancelled in 1997. That was the FIRST time I ever picked up and read a book. (I should note that I had previously opened up coloring books.) That book was *1984* by George Orwell, and it was an assigned reading for English class. For those of you who have never read it, it takes place in a world

THE DEATH OF HUMAN INTERACTION

in which society and government control all. The face of society and government is a character named "Big Brother." Big Brother is never actively present in the story, but he is always watching and controlling. I flipped through that book within a couple days, getting excited each time I turned to the next page both because of the story and because of how the book felt in my hands. The premise was metaphorically based on the controlled world within Nazi Germany where people appeared to be but were not truly free in thought and mind. The society we live in today is different yet the same. Different in the notion that we are not directly controlled by one being, but the same in the sense that we are no longer free in thought. We live in a world of information overload, with ideas, opinions, and advertising abundantly surrounding us and telling us what and how to think. In this world, we are not free thinkers ... we merely resemble them.

While this book is loaded with opinion and some stories here and there, I chose to write it in this format (book as opposed to blog) because I want the next generation to turn off the television, shut down their computer, and open and read a book. I'm writing this as a book because I don't want the next generation to be the "Lost and Never Found Generation." I want to hit them with a simple concept that there is a world beyond electronics that they can escape to. I don't want to offer another link to a flashy blog that is easily accessible. If you want to hear my thoughts and opinions, you are going to have to work for them. But, more importantly, I want to excite the next generation to read books the way that I do, always eager to find the next captivating story. I want to take the opportunity to open their minds and open their hands in the same way that authors like Mr. Orwell did for me (not that I ever deserve to be put into the same conversation as George Orwell).

Just to re-emphasize point 2, it'd be nice if you and all your friends would buy this book. Let's work together to put it on the New York Times *Best Seller List and make me rich! If we do that, I promise to write more books that can hopefully assist with hopes outlined in point 3.*

FORTY
CONCLUSION

The Blame Game/Aaron, The Hypocrite

Every (good?) book must eventually conclude; we are almost there. In my continued attempts to assist those new to reading, I'd like to inform you that this is the last chapter of the book. Once you read the words "The End," there is no more. I want to be absolutely clear on this point to ensure that you do not spend hours, perhaps days, trying to find the pages beyond the end of this chapter; they do not exist. I hope you enjoy a few finals thoughts (and confessions).

We have finally reached the end of this journey (or rant) together. For both of us, this is a monumental moment. For you, you demonstrated that you CAN actually read. For me, I actually completed something I set out to do. Time and time again throughout my life, I told my family I wanted to do this or do that, but I always changed paths (some people might say "quit") not too far into the endeavor.

For example, at one point when I was growing up, I wanted to be a ninja, so I had my parents sign me up for karate classes. After about a month, they bought me a gi and paid for a few more months of classes. Once the slightly longer-term commitment was established (a few months is a long time for a 12-year-old), I got bored and *changed paths*. From the time I was six until I was 10, I wanted to a be a professional baseball player, that was until I got beaned in little league, became afraid to stand in the batter's box, and watched my batting average drop from .400 to .105. I continued with little league for the next couple years but ultimately decided to *change paths.* From my senior year of high school through college graduation, I wanted to be the next big Hollywood producer. Then, after I graduated, I moved to LA to find out that Hollywood sucks (not everything about it, but most aspects). Within a year, I decided to *change paths.* (Mom and Dad, hopefully you can look past all the mean characterizations that I've made of you in this book and take pleasure in the fact that your son actually saw something through!) But enough with my sad story; it's time for the blame game.

As a proud American, I have been trained throughout my existence that in a time of frustration and dissatisfaction, it is important to pass the blame. So I think it is important not to point the finger at my generation or those to follow (if I did, I'd just be blaming myself). We are the victims of a terrible reality that we were born into. It is not our fault that we are obsessed with technology; we have had it at our fingertips from day one. Yes, yes, yes. I agree that my generation has advanced technologies to the point of overkill, but previous generations are the ones who opened the door and pushed us through.

Let's blame the inventors and innovators from Steve Jobs and Bill Gates of my parents' generation to Martin Cooper of my grandparents' generation to the Galvin brothers and Philo Farnsworth (invented television) of my great grandparents'. Let's blame Alexander Graham Bell, Thomas Edison, Benjamin Franklin, and Leonardo Da Vinci. Let's blame the Scottish (my former Scottish roommate once informed me that they "invented the modern world," but I don't buy it!), the Romans, the ancient Greeks, and the ancient Egyptians. Let's blame them all!

It's not my fault that people today cannot hold a conversation. It's not my fault that everyone has the attention of a goldfish. It's not my fault that we have become an obsessed society that no longer knows how to function without its technologies. It's not my fault that the *Death of Human Interaction* is upon us (and if you are part of my generation, it's not your fault either)! IT IS THE FAULT OF EVERYONE THAT CAME BEFORE ME (AND YOU)!

Despite the fact that I am not to blame, I display honor at some point in this book (where better than at the end so that you can remember me as a good guy) and own up to my hypocrisies. To be honest, to some degree it's impossible to survive in today's world without buying into some technologies. To another degree, there are some technologies that are either just plain old cool or absolutely addictive. Before I dismiss class, I'd like to identify several of those hypocrisies (some of which I may have casually owned up to at other points in the book):

1. Since I started writing this book, I've had to be antisocial on more than one occasion. Writing a book while working a full-time job is not an easy task. You have write weeknights and weekends if you ever want to get it done. That means there have been many times when I passed up a friend's barbeque, a baseball game, a hike, LARPing (Google this if you don't know what it is), or a party so that I could sit at my computer in solitude and type some words for you to read. I have made some serious sacrifices for all of you. You are welcome!

2. Several months ago I bought an iPod Touch to replace my five-year-old iPod. When I told my boss, he asked me, "Why the hell did you buy an antiquated technology? Why didn't you just buy an iPhone?" I gave him a similar "I'm above that" type of answer that I gave to many people throughout my last few years of owning a flip phone as opposed to a smart phone. The truth is I think many of the features on an iPhone are pretty cool (especially the games … please refer to chapter 32). I wanted to have the opportunity to play *Angry Birds* like everyone else on the planet (only two years later), but I also didn't want to compromise the stance I had taken on technologies for so long.

I mean, I'm writing a book about gripes with technologies! So I bought an iPod Touch, and, since buying it, I became of those antisocial people on the bus who mostly listens to music and plays video games.

3. I am still a television addict (from time to time, but mostly during the winter).

4. I still watch *The Biggest Loser.*

5. Regarding Facebook: (A) I use it occasionally, but definitely not as much as most. (B) I did remove "single" from my relationship status when I got engaged. (C) Since writing chapter 20, I broke the promise to myself that I would not change my Facebook relationship status to "married" until I either reached 10 years' worth of marriage or three kids; my wife is just too awesome not to tell the world I am married to her.

6. I have previously tried online dating and already admitted to it in chapter 25.

7. Occasionally I turn up the radio volume to shut up one of my two brothers.

8. My mother bought me a GPS as a gift when I moved to San Francisco. I grew addicted to its simplicity and now use it way too much. I'm scared that I'll never get lost again!

9. I still have never used Twitter! (I'm not a hypocrite here; I just wanted to make myself feel good for a moment after all the self-bashing.)

10. I do believe that Wikipedia knows everything and is completely factual!

THE DEATH OF HUMAN INTERACTION

11. I miss the days of Friendster (not MySpace so much).

12. I watch more movies than I read books; Netflix is just so damn easy.

13. I do believe that ChatRoulette was a fun adventure (not really though).

14. I now own an iPad. My mother bought it for my wife and me for Hanukkah to eliminate any excuse not to video chat with her using FaceTime.

15. I decided to start a blog since writing chapter 39. It is called the "The Life of Panz." I created it in the winter of 2011 and by the spring of 2014 I intend to post to it at least once.

THE END

THANK YOU

Taking this booked from concept to publication was not a quick or easy process. It took me multiple years and required a lot of support, patience, and inspiration from many people… family, friends, and strangers.

First of all, thank you to my mother. You were a key inspiration for me writing this book and you know why. I love you very much and appreciate that you won't disown me once a few people that you know read the book.

Thank you to all of my other family – Dad, Marc, Jeff, and my extended family - and friends that supported me along the way, especially those who exhibited excitement for the topic and encouraged me to keep going during times when I was slowed down. Many of you helped me through this book both by sharing ideas, reviewing certain chapters, giving me your honest feedback, and making me feel like I am somewhat funny.

Thank you to all of the strangers I met at coffee shops while writing this books that allowed me to either interrupt you to get your opinion. Thank you to all of the strangers on the buses, planes, trains, etc., who allowed me to observe your ridiculous behaviors to inspire new ideas for the book. I couldn't have written this book without you!

Finally, thank you to my beautiful and loving wife, Katie. Thank you for always being so supportive of all of my crazy ambitions in life. I'm thrilled that we're on this ride today. Also, I know that I did omit a couple of chapters from this book per your preference. Though I may have put up a small argument to keep them in there, I think the book overall is better without them. Here it is in writing for the world to see... You were right!

ABOUT THE AUTHOR

Aaron Panzer was born in a hospital in a town to two parents and four grandparents. His mother gave birth to him, and his father donated to the cause.

He has previously read books and enjoyed them. Aaron is also the author of future books for which he has yet to develop ideas. You will find them on bookshelves at Barnes & Noble and Borders and on Amazon.com within the next 30 years (the amount of time it took him to write this one), assuming these retailers still exist in due time. (Since I began writing, Borders did, in fact, go out of business,) If not, please find an alternative method to obtain his books.

www.ingramcontent.com/pod-product-compliance
Lightning Source LLC
Chambersburg PA
CBHW031441040426
42444CB00007B/918